The Enneagram
for Moms

The Enneagram for Moms

See the True Colors of Yourself and

Your Children as God Intends

Beth McCord

with Lydia J. Craig and John Driver

W PUBLISHING GROUP

AN IMPRINT OF THOMAS NELSON

The Enneagram for Moms

© 2024 Beth McCord and Jeff McCord

Published in Nashville, Tennessee, by W Publishing, an imprint of Thomas Nelson.

Published in association with the literary agency of Wolgemuth & Wilson.

Thomas Nelson titles may be purchased in bulk for educational, business, fundraising, or sales promotional use. For information, please email SpecialMarkets@ThomasNelson.com.

ISBN 978–0-7852-9109-1 (audiobook)
ISBN 978–0-7852-9107-7 (ePub)
ISBN 978–0-7852-9106-0 (SC)

Library of Congress Control Number: 2024930967

Printed in the United States of America
24 25 26 27 28 LBC 5 4 3 2 1

For all the moms who feel they don't have enough time, energy, wisdom, or ability to navigate the ever-changing wonder and challenge of motherhood.

I hope these pages offer you rest, hope, and a path forward as your truest self.

Contents

Part 2

Introduction

Made Just for Moms

You're a mom, just like me.

This means it's not very hard to imagine where you are right now. From toddler to teenager to every stage in between, you are right in the middle of it, whatever "it" may be. Diapers and driving lessons. Ball games and biology. Laundry and LEGO blocks. Refereeing and . . . well, refereeing (this one deserves two mentions, right?). Endless chores, Band-Aids, homework, driving, cooking. And yes, endless waiting and worrying, desperately hoping you are somehow meeting a thousand spoken and unspoken expectations, though you're probably not very convinced.

Sound familiar? I hope so, because I wrote this book just for you.

I am a mom, but I'm also the founder of Your Enneagram Coach. Our company produces resources and trains certified Enneagram coaches to help hundreds of thousands of people better understand their own motivations and patterns using the tool of the Enneagram. We help people of all ages and backgrounds, including moms like you.

But since you're a mom, we don't have any time to waste—so let's cut to the chase! I hope these pages will become a sanctuary where you can find moments of rest and encouragement. Yes, I know that you love your kids and deeply enjoy the adventure of raising them through these precious, fleeting years and stages. But I also know what it's like to be exhausted and overwhelmed before 6:00 a.m.

Motherhood is an experience like no other, so I invite you to join me on a different kind of reading journey—one that is to-the-point, full of grace, free of comparisons, and shockingly simple and effective.

Together, we will discover valuable tools to help our children navigate their own emotional landscapes with self-awareness and resilience. My hope is that this book becomes an essential resource that speaks directly to the heart of any mother, caregiver, or concerned adult seeking guidance and peace—that is, to *your* heart.

Your heart is one thing, but your hectic schedule is another. That's why I have written this book to be different from most, even in its format. Instead of feeling the pressure to find thirty or forty-five minutes to finish a typical chapter, I have written this book with much shorter chapters. That's right, part 1 of this book is made up of fifteen short, readable chapters. I wrote this with you in mind as you hide away for five or ten minutes during a nap time (that will most likely get cut way too short) or as you wait in the car line for school to end.

I also want to offer you a treasure trove of practical applications in the latter section of this book. There you will find visual aids, lists, and descriptions that can be easily accessed and understood as you ponder and work through the simple concepts we are about to discuss. Trust me, you will want to turn to part 2 (if you haven't already) and return there over and over again. That's what these sections are there for, so we needn't fake like we're people who don't flip to the back of books before finishing the front. This is your book and your parenting journey. Be free!

Obviously, the idea of being a mom means different things to different people, but throughout my interactions with thousands of mothers who listen to our podcasts, attend our events, or engage in our coaching communities, I have found that most of us have a few things in common. We often wonder (if only to ourselves), *Why am I losing my patience so quickly? Why do I feel so much shame when my family isn't behaving in an "ideal" way? Why does one of my kids withdraw and the other become unreasonable and combative? Am I crazy?*

Depending on who you are, these questions probably land on you in vastly different ways. However, most moms do not know why they think, feel, or respond to the beauty and challenge of parenting in the specific ways they do—ways that are different from other moms and also different from their kids. That's where I hope to help.

We need help because parenting is like adding our own contribution to a vibrant and intricate work of art, full of colorful challenges and unexpected joys. In a world where being a mom can feel like a chaotic and unpredictable journey, it's no surprise that so many moms seek answers and solutions through endless online content promising relief to parents searching for ways to nurture their children's health, growth, and resiliency. But these promises do not always produce the same reactions or results in each of us. This is because we are not all the same—we are different in significant ways that can be explored and known. Understanding how we are different is more important than you might realize.

But for all the ways we are different, we are all moms. That's why I wrote this book just for you. If you're ready, let's get started on this journey together.

Part 1

CHAPTER 1

No Day at the Park

It was supposed to be a fun day on the playground. My kids, Nate and Libby, were still young enough to be wholly overtaken by wonder and excitement at the mere thought of swinging on the swings and sliding down the slides. I really wanted to join in on the fun, to be present with them in the moment, but I just couldn't.

I was stuck.

As I watched the other moms interact with their children, I couldn't help but feel a mix of admiration and envy. They seemed to effortlessly embody all the qualities of the mother I wanted to be. Some were creative and could come up with imaginative games on the spot. Some had a natural knack for making their kids laugh with their funny antics. Others had a remarkable ability to connect with even the littlest ones, making them feel safe and loved. And then there were those who exuded humble confidence, leading their children with grace and wisdom.

But as I stood there surrounded by these incredible moms, doubts and insecurities flooded my mind. The weight of comparison pressed upon me, and I couldn't shake the feeling that I fell short in every way. Despite putting on a brave face, I was battling a storm within.

Everyone—even the other moms on the playground—seemed to be certain about what it takes to be a good mom. They appeared to have it all together, radiating patience, kindness, and a deep understanding of their children. In contrast, I felt overwhelmed, inadequate, and powerless. Scarcity, insecurity, and shame filled my thoughts, and I became my harshest critic, haunted by a relentless inner monologue that highlighted my perceived shortcomings as a mother. *Those other moms are not a mess on the inside like you because you have no idea what you're doing. You're the only one who is so frustrated and scared about your kids. What's wrong with you?*

Apart from the moms I could see on the playground, my mind was also reeling from the endless input and ideas of numerous expert authors and influencers, along with many well-meaning friends. Instead of making me feel better and better equipped, I wanted to withdraw, hide, and give up. Each piece of seemingly foolproof advice sounded right, but this overload of information was not bringing me peace. Quite the opposite. *If you don't discipline enough, your kids will become spoiled and resistant to authority. But wait, if you discipline too much, your kids will emotionally detach from you and spend the rest of their lives unable to sustain close relationships. Also, sleep schedules work—until they don't, and your child becomes unable to adapt outside of a rigid routine. You should let your children make more choices for themselves. But also, your children can become overwhelmed and develop anxiety from making too many choices too early. So go ahead and step up as their mom . . . but just know, you're doing it wrong!*

With so many voices clouding my mind, my confidence was shattered, and it felt like I was losing my own voice. My inner world as a young mom was spinning out of control in ways I could not understand in the moment, much less articulate.

Above all, I felt alone.

The playground, a place meant for connection and shared experiences, had become an inner battleground of comparison and self-condemnation. I longed to ask for help, advice, and insight from the other moms, but I feared judgment and the whispers of gossip that might ensue if my struggles were exposed. Little did I know that behind their composed facades, those very same moms were wrestling with their own hidden battles. We were all trapped in a cycle of striving and pretending, yearning for acceptance and validation.

Still, amid the chaos of my emotions, there was a glimmer of hope.

It came later that evening after we were home from the playground. The kids were all down for the night, but my inner tension was only ramping up. I wanted to hide it from my husband, Jeff, embarrassed that such deep insecurities and doubts had overtaken me even though nothing was seriously wrong with our beautiful family. But Jeff saw me—and as it turned out, he could also see through the fog that had me lost and disoriented. Sometimes, it takes someone or something outside of ourselves to help us stop being blind to what is staring us right in the face.

With love and wisdom, Jeff gently pointed out how I had unknowingly crafted a mythical figure in my mind: the supermom. She was an ideal that no one, not even myself, could attain. He also reminded me that I had my own set of gifts, abilities, and limitations. Instead of trying to conform to an unreachable standard, he encouraged me to embrace my true self, even as I celebrated the unique qualities of other women.

Jeff's insights began to shatter the illusion I had created, setting me on a transformative journey. It was here, at rock bottom, that I began reaching up and reaching out for help, which led me to a tool called the Enneagram.

What Is the Enneagram?

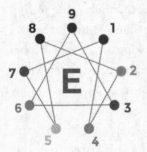

Enneagram comes from the Greek words *ennea* ("nine") and *gramma* ("diagram)."
It is a map or GPS for self-discovery and personal growth based on nine basic personality types. The Enneagram clearly describes why people think, feel, and behave based upon four core motivations.

We are always trying to fulfill our core longing (the message our heart longs to hear). But in the process, we are also running away from our type's core fear (what we're trying to prevent from happening), running toward our type's core desire (what we're striving to obtain), and stumbling over our type's core weakness (the issue our personality always struggles with).

Our four core motivations are the driving forces behind *why* we think, feel, and behave in particular ways. By understanding our core motivations, we can understand why we do what we do and learn to navigate our inner world in the best direction for our personality type.

The tool of the Enneagram helped me better understand myself—my innate beauty and strengths, as well as the negative messages and patterns that were most affecting me, particularly in my role as a parent. If I didn't learn to better understand the way I was made, I would forever be stuck in these negative messages. I would believe them to be true and to be the only ways to see myself, my children, and the world around me.

That difficult day at the park—where I was filled with envy and self-doubt—marked the beginning of a profound shift in my perspective as a mother. It ignited a desire to help other moms break free from the cycles of comparison and unrealistic expectations. Almost twenty-five years later, I am still on this transformative path, sharing my journey and offering guidance to mothers who long to find confidence and peace amid the beautiful messiness of motherhood. I still get spun out as a parent, so if you're looking for an expert mom with perfect kids and all the right answers, you've come to the wrong woman. But what I have found is more confidence and peace in my journey and role as a mom. You can too.

The cycles of mommy shaming and mommy guilting are hard to break because being a mom isn't always a day at the park. Let me offer you hope, because motherhood is divinely intended to be a transformative journey where moms not only help paint a portrait of a healthy, thriving family (more on this soon) but also cultivate resilience, self-awareness, and deep connections with God, their spouse (if applicable), and their children. You no longer have to strive for perfection by attempting to meet society's expectations of you, or for that matter, your own insecure standards of comparison. You can begin to navigate the beautiful messiness of family life with a deeper understanding of your unique inner world.

So pull up a swing and sit awhile with me. You're not alone in this park.

CHAPTER 2

Understanding True Colors

In the beginning, God created many things—the sky, the earth, the animals that inhabit it. But these things were not all the same shape, size, or color. They were diverse, and together, they painted the world in blues and greens and many other colors. I like to think that the Enneagram represents that same creative, colorful approach to people.

If you've ever had your family sit for a professional photograph, then you know it's quite an experience. It takes lots of primping, fidgeting, and repositioning to get just the right shot, with everyone in the family actually looking at the camera. But can you imagine living in the 1700s and having your family sit for an actual painted portrait? That's a long time for kids to sit still!

It's one thing to think about sitting still for a physical photo or portrait (or at least trying to), but what if your family's crazy everyday life is also painting a picture of sorts? You could think of yourself, your kids, and everyone in your life as their own completely unique color being added to a canvas. The colors are vivid and diverse, being graciously blended to create the beautiful messiness of family life. With each conversation, each event, and each reaction in your lives together, your family story is being painted. Right now. And as a mom, you get to help hold the brush. Now imagine that the nine Enneagram types make up this vibrant palette of different colors, each shade representing a unique personality with its own perspectives, motivations, and strategies. Just as an artist selects specific colors to create a masterpiece, God uses each Enneagram type to bring a distinct hue to the canvas of his creation. Learning more about your Enneagram personality type means learning more about who you really are; that is, your true colors.

How Do I Find My Enneagram Type?

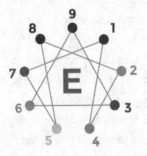

Taking our online Enneagram assessment is a great starting point. All well-done Enneagram tests are about 80 percent accurate because they are trying to assess your vast inner world. This means that your results will depend on how well you know yourself and what is currently going on in your life. It's best to answer the questions based on how you've historically approached life, not how you feel in this particular moment.

You can find our assessment at EnneagramForMoms.com. Since tests are not 100 percent accurate, we encourage you to also read all nine types' core motivations. You can download and print the nine types' core motivations at EnneagramForMoms.com in the Free Resources section. If you relate to more than one personality type, try "wearing one" for a few days to see if the core motivations genuinely reflect your inner thoughts and emotions. Our Mistyping Guide can further help you understand the key difference between any two Enneagram types. You can also download the Mistyping Guide in the Free Resources section. Eventually, you will narrow it down to one type, which we refer to as your main type.

But if you get stuck, the most insightful way to discover your main type is to have an expert guide navigate you through the process. You can do this by researching and connecting with your own certified Enneagram coach from our free list of coaches at EnneagramForMoms.com.

Whether you are new to the Enneagram or an experienced enthusiast, I promise you can still grasp the simple concept of finding your true colors. For now, just think of Type One as a shade of blue, Type Two as a shade of teal, Type Three as a dark green, and so forth for all nine types, with each type having its own color that reflects certain core motivations and strategies that we will unpack in the pages to come. (You can see how the image of Your Enneagram Coach's logo on the back cover reflects these different colors for different types.)

Thinking of Enneagram types as colors is a powerful approach that can help us grasp the intricacies of human personality and interaction. Just as each color adds depth and dimension to a painting, each Enneagram type brings their unique strengths and challenges to the painted tapestry of our family life. By recognizing these colors within ourselves and others, we can gain a deeper understanding of our motivations, thinking patterns, and ways of relating to each other and the world.

But let us not forget that these colors are not static or limiting. They are merely the starting point of self-awareness and growth. Each type represents a rich spectrum of shades and nuances, just as each person within a type is a unique blend of colors. No two individuals of the same type are exactly alike. They each bring their own life experiences, talents, and perspectives to the canvas. Your precise personality and overall personhood are like no one else's. You are your own divinely tinted shade.

I am an Enneagram Type Nine (the Peaceful Accommodator). This means that my core fear is being in conflict, feeling shut out and overlooked, or losing connection and relationship with others. The Nine's core desire is to have inner stability and peace of mind, which is connected to our core longing to hear that our presence and voice matters.

At Your Enneagram Coach, we represent this type by using the color purple in our logo. There are many other Type Nines out there, but none of us is exactly the same shade of purple since we each have different strengths, weaknesses, talents, traumas, and stories. Even so, we do still share certain motivations, thought patterns, strategies, and overall perspectives for approaching our lives. We can learn a lot about ourselves and others who fall on this continuum of Type Nines by studying the Enneagram.

As a mom, it can get a little more complicated, of course. While you have a certain Enneagram type, your kids were also born with a main Enneagram type—a distinct color, if you will. Within them already exists a certain way of seeing and interacting with the world based on their main Enneagram type. It's important to note that Enneagram wisdom leans away from attempting to assign a type to a child (or anyone for that matter) because each person must be the one to discover their main type by finding and articulating what core motivations are driving why they think, feel, and behave the way they do. This means we have to wait until children are old enough to more fully understand themselves (their core motivations). Kids are still learning and developing in their self-awareness; therefore, we must be patient and curious until they are old enough to declare the type they identify as their main Enneagram type, which is usually in their teenage years or older. For some, it can take a long time to discover, and that is perfectly normal.

That's why this book will *not* be about figuring out every aspect of your kid's Enneagram type. Rather, I will give you insight into ways to remain curious and responsive to the various emerging tones of your child's unique shading, whether they are an infant or a teenager driving your car.

As we explore the different types, you'll discover a major truth about the true colors concept: you are different from your child. Of course, we already know this on an intellectual level, but as parents, our emotional frustrations often bypass our intellect. Without realizing it, we can expect our kids to show up in the world thinking, feeling, and behaving just like us. We generally consider the ways we do things to be the right ways, which is why we do them. So naturally, we want our children to do the same. When our kids show up differently, it can make us feel confused, frustrated, disappointed, and even angry—and that's not fair to them. We need to either discover for the first time or once again remember that everyone, including our children, is different. They have their own unique way of being in the world apart from your way.

Everyone has their own true colors.

This is why the Enneagram is so helpful. It is simply a tool that offers a better understanding of someone's perceptions, motivations, thinking and feeling patterns, defensive strategies, unique strengths, and way of relating to the world. We may already know what we do, but the Enneagram helps us better understand *why* we do it. It helps us learn more about our true personality type. And even if we can't type our children, we can become more attuned to their emotional and thinking patterns.

In my own story, as I began to grow in my understanding of my motivations, I realized that I was making the same mistake I previously mentioned: I assumed that my kids needed to see and react to the world as I do—that is, like a Type Nine. I was trying to get my kids to become a mini-version of me by insisting that they always be kind, peaceable, accommodating, and easygoing. In essence, I tried to "paint over" my children's unique colors with my own. It was only natural for me to assume that "purple" (my unique internal makeup as a Type Nine) was the best color—or in some cases, the only correct color—with which to paint. What I didn't fully realize or understand at the time was that each of my kids already had their own unique color (Enneagram personality type) that had yet to fully emerge.

To better understand this concept, let's go back in time to when my daughter, Libby, was six years old. She wanted to paint her room a new color. We went to the paint store for her to pick out the color that would soon cover her walls. The reason I will never forget this experience is not because she picked out the most hideous color, Kermit-the-Frog green, but because of the fascinating process by which the color came into being in the paint can. Have you ever seen this process happen at a paint store? If not, I highly recommend that you go and watch it happen.

Each color comes with a unique code to give the person behind the counter instructions for mixing. When they remove the lid on the can of base paint, it is completely white. The specialist adds whatever combination of colors the code calls for, but these drop straight to the bottom and settle beneath the base, just waiting to be mixed. Before the mixing occurs, the paint can, though it contains colors, still looks plain white. The true colors are there; you just can't see them yet.

Now imagine that you walk into the paint store and instead of getting to pick the color you desire, you are handed a can of white paint without knowing that a very specific and unique combination of colors has already been added to it. Again, this is because the colors reside on the bottom in a way you can't see. They haven't yet been mixed. This is what it's like to become a parent.

When our children enter our lives, we don't yet know who they are or who they will become. We don't realize that they have a very specific personality type already placed within them that over the course of time will emerge through the mixing of life experiences, self-awareness, and maturity. Therefore, when they are born and lie so little and helpless in our arms, we falsely assume that their personality is like this unmixed can of paint that looks white. We assume they are ready for us to add our own personality traits, core motivations, and ways of seeing and interacting with the world to them. So as we begin raising them, we try to add our own color, using whatever "stir sticks" we already have—parenting techniques and strategies that consciously or unconsciously reflect our own Enneagram type's motivations. We attempt to morph our kids into the main color on the palette we know best: our own.

Then something unexpected happens. Our children begin exhibiting behaviors and ways of thinking that don't align with our own. In these moments, we are tempted to assume our way is superior and prejudge their actions as wrong. I often hear from moms who feel perplexed and frustrated when their children express unfamiliar beliefs and messages, wondering how these thoughts got there, especially when they know they were not introduced by the parents. It's like they are saying: *Wait, I thought this was a can of plain white paint! Where are all these other colors coming from that clash so much with mine?*

The most important thing to realize is that your child's unique personality is not a problem. It is a reflection of the way they are designed. As moms, we can let go of trying to fully control our kids' lives and personalities, which means we can also let go of all our anxious fears that they will clash with (or at least not match) our own colors.

Understanding the Enneagram can provide clarity. Each Enneagram type carries its unique set of messages, perceptions, and strategies that children naturally lean on, especially since they generally lack awareness or the ability to change them. Just like us as moms, our kids will naturally begin acting and reacting based on their Enneagram type's preprogrammed way of seeing the world. They may look like white paint, but their true colors will eventually show up whether they (or we) are aware of them or not. And this will also color what they see and believe about themselves and the world around them.

CHAPTER 3

The Lenses That Color
Our Stories

I have come to better understand that an ever-growing awareness of my true personality's colors and how they affect my children is closely tied to my story. This is true for everyone. The very concept of a story is shaped by where we are born, the value systems of our parents, the victories and traumas we have experienced, and a million other details that comprise the narrative of a life. But our life's external story is actually a part of something bigger. Each one of us also has our own internal (or developmental) story that is informed not just by our experiences but also by our Enneagram type.

As we explored in the previous chapter, our Enneagram types have been with us since birth, gradually emerging through our personalities. These colors also seep into the lenses through which we view and experience the world, affecting how we understand it and our role within it. It's like we've been wearing glasses tinted with the color of our personality type since birth, even though we may not have been aware of it. Our type's unique colored lens, whether it's blue, purple, red, or another shade, has been our primary way of making sense of ourselves, others, and the world around us. Our personality's distinct perspective has played a significant role in shaping us and the way we see our stories—that is, what we believe about ourselves and the world.

In *Parenting from the Inside Out,* Daniel Siegel, MD, and Mary Hartzell, MEd, lay out a compelling framework for the way our inner work as parents affects our kids' developmental stories. You'll notice that I will refer to their book multiple times, alongside other key sources. This is because their concepts parallel many of the ones we will be applying as we learn more about our true personality types. They write, "Stories are the way we make sense of the events of our lives. Individually and collectively, we tell stories in order to understand what has happened to us and to create meaning from those experiences."[1]

As our kids grow, we witness this process as they clumsily try to understand their lives and identities. Much of the distress they experience arises from new, ever-emerging internal messages and beliefs that are based on core motivations, thought patterns, and perspectives of their yet-to-be-discovered Enneagram type. The messages and beliefs that come from their personality type directly tint their unique personality's lens, influencing their developmental stories. Their stories are still being written, but even at a young age, they carry and experience very specific internal narratives.

If you're a parent with multiple children, you're probably already well aware of how your kids naturally have diverse perspectives on the world. One might appear confident and eager to take on challenges, while another may seem reserved and anxious, doubting their abilities to tackle those challenges. Regardless of the situation, each child views the world through a preset personality lens that shapes their outlook based on their personality's internal narratives. And as I said in the previous chapter, your child's unique way of looking at themselves and the world isn't a problem on its own. There are no good or bad Enneagram types; every type can operate in both healthy and unhealthy ways.

Again, we can think of each type as having a color associated with it. For example, we can assign the color blue to Type One and the color orange to Type Six. Now imagine that each type wears their own pair of glasses with these colored lenses. The Type One is wearing blue-tinted glasses, while Type Six is wearing orange-tinted glasses. Both types can experience the same circumstance, but each will perceive it, interpret it, and react differently based on their personality's unique perspective.

In addition to how they see and engage with the world, how they do this can range from healthy to unhealthy, depending on their internal state. When a person is in a healthy state, they'll see through their type's color lens in a brighter, healthier way. But when they're struggling or less healthy, their lens will have a darker tint, affecting how they perceive and interact with the world in less healthy ways. In an unhealthy state, they might start believing negative and untrue things about themselves, others, and life. However, when they're healthy, they'll see life's truths and approach it with a healthier perspective, radiating positivity and brightness for all to benefit from.

In many ways, I just described the very essence of childhood. Kids constantly find themselves living in the tension of what version of truth they should believe about their own internal narratives. They are not only hearing messages from external sources like parents, teachers, and the world, but also from within. On any given day, each type can wrestle with many competing thoughts like:

Type One: *I must not make any mistakes in order to be good and right.*

Type Two: *I must help others in order to be loved and wanted.*

Type Three: *I must achieve success in order to be admired and valued.*

Type Four: *I must not be too much or not enough in order to be fully known and loved for my unique self.*

Type Five: *I must not withdraw too much even though alone time comforts me and helps me recharge my internal energy reserves.*

Type Six: *I must not trust myself but find trusted authorities who will guide me and keep me safe and secure.*

Type Seven: *I must not rely on anyone but myself to find complete satisfaction in my life.*

Type Eight: *I must not trust anyone but myself to protect me.*

Type Nine: *I must not assert myself but instead go along with others to ensure peace and harmony.*

It's no wonder our kids spin out into emotional dysregulation on a regular basis, with so many highs and lows. The emergence of their unique personality traits can be quite overwhelming and frightening for them, leaving them uncertain about their true selves and which narrative they should believe and embrace.

As we grow and develop, our ability to emotionally regulate ourselves depends on various factors, including our age and the nurturing we receive. Unlike most adults, children lack the cognitive ability and self-awareness to regulate themselves effectively and will naturally react to situations based on their personality's raw perceptions and experiences. In light of these challenges, it's vital for us to learn to approach our children with curiosity and non-accusatory questions, demonstrating our desire to understand and support them from their unique personality bent—or better said, their personality tint. After all, they are only trying to understand themselves within their developing story that is still unfolding. But please know that having patience, gaining understanding, and asking curious questions as we experience our kids on their own journey of self-awareness can be quite challenging for moms as well. Along with our children, we can also struggle to understand their developing stories.

As mothers, each of us also carries our own internal stories, which usually differ from our children's, even when faced with similar situations. This is why through the lens of our own unique stories and personalities, our children's developing narratives may appear disconcerting to us. Their divergences from our ways of seeing things can trigger emotions like confusion, fear, or reactivity within us. You're probably reading this book because you've experienced such emotions. But is there anything we can truly do to address these feelings? Yes, there is.

The truth is, as moms, we're on a journey *with* our children as they discover their developmental stories. We are not writing their stories; we are a part of them. This means we are not in control. I personally have found comfort in knowing that God already knows their story because he sees the end just as clearly as the beginning, which means he truly has the end in mind—and it's for their ultimate good. When I began to rest in this, I learned that it was possible to stop being so overcome with fear, anxiety, or a desire for control. Even though our kids' lenses can look so unrecognizable and unpredictable compared to our own, we can hold on to hope as we also learn to keep a positive end in mind.

In their journey, there may be challenges, but we can cultivate a calm, non-anxious, and connected presence that reassures our children. Yes, it's possible. But how? That is an important question leading to the most critical step so far. The truth is, while we often try to understand our children's inner worlds and stories in order to guide or correct them, the most significant impact on our children's well-being actually comes from whether we, as moms, become aware of our own selves first. We must explore and understand our own unique developmental stories. Our colored lens, not theirs, is where we must begin.

CHAPTER 4

Why You Need to Start with You

"Nate! You stop yelling and chasing your sister! Right now!"

Nate was at *that* age. You know, the one where you still acknowledge their half birthday to somehow convince yourself that your kids' current stage, even if you appreciate many parts of it, surely cannot last much longer.

As a three-and-half-year-old, Nate was merely doing what kids in the "half years" do. This was not surprising. What was surprising is that his adult mother had just leapt a baby gate like an Olympic hurdler, screaming at the top of her lungs as she ungracefully chased her son around the toy-filled room. I was determined to put a stop to his behavior, insisting that he treat his little sister, Libby, with patience, kindness, and grace.

In McCord family legend, the comically chaotic episode became known as "Babygate." It was quite a scene, and somewhere in the madness of the moment, God opened my eyes to the fact that I was acting in the very way I was demanding that Nate should change. My reaction stemmed from my Type Nine's desire that everyone be treated kindly. Unaware of the reasons behind my reactions, I failed to remain mindful and composed, letting my unhelpful overreactions take control. No matter what I was hollering at the time, I inadvertently taught Nate that chasing and yelling were acceptable actions, reinforcing the very behavior I sought to prevent.

Before our kids came into our lives, I had this picture-perfect idea of how I was going to parent and shape my kids. Have you done this as well? If so, have you ever noticed that your vision of how you want your kids to be shaped matches your personality type? Well, this was absolutely true for me. In fact, everything I was trying to instill in my kids came directly from my Type Nine perspective. I dreamt of us spending quality time together, growing and learning as a family while building strong, harmonious bonds. We would have a home where we played lots of board games together, enjoyed long talks around a cozy dinner table, and cuddled up to read stories before bedtime. In my dreams, I thought my parenting style would foster kind, empathetic, and peaceful children—with me, of course, forging the path ahead as their loving, yet reasonably assertive guide. I was convinced I was going to bring this vision to reality. How could my vision not happen? It seemed easy enough, right?

I honestly believed I knew how to create little peaceful accommodators. (The next chapter will describe the parenting expectations of each Enneagram type, so hang tight.) But of course, reality pelted my expectations with a rotating supply of dirty diapers, unhappy kids, and soiled bibs. My perfect vision was dismantled right out of the gate since Nate suffered from colic throughout his entire first year. Nothing I tried seemed to make a difference. Libby wasn't colicky her first year, but she wanted my attention and physical presence constantly. As my vision became a long-lost dream, my patience began to dwindle, leaving me irritable and moody.

What were your visions and expectations before your kids entered your life? Can you see how they correlate with your main type's ways of seeing and relating to the world?

As my kids transitioned into their toddler years, I finally took the fantasy portrait down from the mental wall, sadly conceding to the disheartening fact that they weren't going to follow my lead without questioning, whining, and challenging me. Day-to-day power struggles left me feeling frustrated, overwhelmed, and utterly drained. I couldn't fathom why I couldn't achieve the harmonious family life I'd imagined. It seemed so doable. Where had I gone wrong?

As I look back on those early years (and the stages after), parenting was incredibly tough. Trust me, if other moms around you or on social media describe parenting only as "magical," let me be the first to tell you that you're not a bad mom if you don't find every moment to be enchanted with sugar plums and pixie dust. Being a mom is both beautiful and hard. Perhaps, as you read this, you're trying to enjoy a five-minute escape—a respite from irritability, frustration, disappointment, or guilt marked by yelling, overreacting, criticizing, withdrawing, or crying. If so, please know that you're in good company. I went through (and sometimes still go through) these same emotions, feeling desperate to find new ways to understand and connect with my children, ways that would somehow make parenting easier.

But my Babygate moment was a much-needed wake-up call to a different journey toward self-awareness as a parent, one informed by my main Enneagram type. I wish I could say that I instantly became a perfect parent, but it doesn't work that way. Even so, despite my many ongoing mistakes, I committed to learning from them, growing as a person, and developing stronger relationships with my kids based on more than just the primary ways I see and interact with the world. How did I find this path? I didn't. God's love was the path that found me. It led me to begin focusing on self-awareness, compassionate communication, and grace-filled conflict resolution. Much of what led me into these deeper ways was learned the hard way over many years. I want to help you skip the learning curve and get right to the heart of these essential skills that are found in becoming aware of your main Enneagram type.

In the all-too-common parental drive to shape or "fix" our kids, moms, like me, often overlook the real issue we are facing: we have not yet learned to recognize and regulate our own inner worlds. We are not aware of our own true colors. In other words, we don't understand our own personality type and its unique core motivations, which also means we have not yet unpacked or become familiar with our own internal story.

Contrary to what we feel, the single most important variable in the parenting journey is not nailing down all that is wrong or needs to be adjusted with our kids. Rather, it is learning to make sense of our own internal worlds. Again, Siegel and Hartzell write, "The best predictor of a child's security of attachment to a caregiver is the way that adult has made sense of his or her own childhood experiences."[2] This means a mom's capacity to be aware of her child's developing mind and emotions is directly and deeply related to whether she herself has first addressed her own developmental story. For adults, this means learning to acknowledge and find healing for our own emotional patterns, memories, and traumas.

Specifically, we can move closer to healing when we begin learning to see our own developmental story—including our memories and trauma—through the lens of our type. After all, our type saw and interpreted each of our experiences in unique ways. This new awareness will greatly help us to understand why different circumstances had a particular impact on our hearts in the ways they did.

Whether we know it or not, these issues of self-awareness and self-understanding are already affecting the ways we are showing up in our kids' lives. In fact, they are much more significant than the number of parenting books we read, the chore charts we create, or the well-meaning lectures we dictate to our children. This is why I want to help you primarily focus on recognizing how your own Enneagram type manifests in your life. Then, together, we can walk toward becoming healthier—and extending that health to our children.

If we can learn and grow in this area, it will help us become calm and steady as we show up in our kids' lives as a humble, curious, non-anxious, connected presence. However, lacking self-awareness and never learning to know ourselves well can create unhealthy dynamics and problems for ourselves and our kids. Our issues can begin mixing with theirs, making it especially hard for our children to keep developing into their own unique selves.

Trying to raise our children into little replicas of ourselves is an option most moms try at one point or another—I know I did. But if we haven't dealt with our emotions and experiences, we may unknowingly transfer our most negative traits onto our children. Furthermore, when parents are not emotionally healthy, it can lead to a cycle where the child's issues trigger the parent's unresolved problems, creating an unhelpful dynamic that resurfaces from the parent's early, unresolved story. This is how parents can pass on their unhealthy coping mechanisms to their children.

Instead of fighting against or ignoring our own stories that help make sense of the ways our internal worlds are naturally organized, which often leads to conflicts within our families, we can embrace them and begin parenting as our truest selves. This will also keep us from trying to make our kids little versions of us. Of course, this cannot happen if we never become aware of how our Enneagram types are already showing up in our own lives, much less our kids'. Awareness is where we must begin, which includes examining where we came from.

When I was in the thick of parenting little kids, I didn't know that I was subconsciously responding to the difficulty by repeating patterns from my own childhood, which was perpetuating generational issues that had been passed down to me. But I did this in my own type's unique way related to how I was parented as a kid. As Siegel and Hartzell reveal, "If we have leftover or unresolved issues, it is crucial that we take the time to pause and reflect on our emotional responses to our children. By understanding ourselves we give our children the chance to develop their own sense of vitality and the freedom to experience their own emotional worlds without restrictions and fear."[3] We must learn more about what has been passed down to us and how we uniquely process it.

An important aside here: my heart goes out to anyone who faced things in their childhood that they can't "just get over." There was no excuse for anyone abusing or neglecting you in your childhood or adulthood. This is not your fault or yours to fix. However, there is healing you can pursue. I encourage you to enlist the help of an excellent mental health practitioner as you take this journey. In fact, I highly recommend that at some point in our lives, everyone should find a trusted professional with whom they can truly unpack their story in ways that will cultivate healing, growth, and resilience.

Wherever you are as a mom, you've probably had your own "hurdle the baby gate to chase Nate" moment. Whatever it is for you, I invite you to embrace the unpredictable parts of the parenting story unfolding all around you. In my case, these experiences confronted me with a choice: I could either wallow in guilt and self-blame, spiraling into a cycle of shame, or I could accept the situation and learn from it. The latter has brought great awareness, healing, and growth for myself and my family. I wish the same for you.

CHAPTER 5

Perfection and Expectation

In the past, the expectations of motherhood were based upon one's immediate surroundings—what they saw and experienced in their own families and local communities. But through the proliferation of social media, reality television, YouTube, and the like, we're now bombarded with "expert" opinions from around the world. Even when seemingly sound advice is offered on these mediums, a scroll through the comments reveals endless streams of shame, judgment, and contempt.

Despite a seemingly ever-moving target of right and wrong, often proclaimed as whatever each of us deems these to be for ourselves, society still holds to hidden standards that most mothers cannot attain, with little room allowed for making mistakes and learning from them. Certain mistakes make us "bad" or "toxic" moms—such as what we're feeding our kids, how much screen time we allow, what activities we choose, or what we're teaching or not teaching our children. The target may be moving, but it does still exist. The world is happy to point out when a mother is wrong, even if the world can't agree on a definition of wrong itself.

This moving target is partly the result of us—though usually subconsciously—bringing our own Enneagram-driven expectations to parenting. Even if we are insecure as parents, we still tend to instinctively believe that our approach is the right one—that is, we see the world through the lens of a certain color, but we don't realize it because we've only ever seen it that way. This makes it easy to judge others who do things differently, even though such a mindset contributes to the overall shaming tone society directs at moms. We often don't even know we are doing it as we float along in the same currents of widespread criticism toward other moms. And of course, sometimes we are prone to drown *ourselves* in these currents of mommy shame.

The tension we all feel over the "correct" ways to parent arises from two things: our own developmental stories, and the fact that each Enneagram type has a set of ideals and expectations we want our children to live up to. We work tirelessly to instill these values, often asleep within us, into our children.

We've already explained the impact of our developmental stories, and in a later chapter, we will help you acknowledge the ways that past harms may be affecting your parenting. In this chapter, I'd like to take a moment to explore the various Enneagram types at play in our parenting expectations. We are so deeply informed by our Enneagram type that we can feel our children are flawed or inadequate if they don't fully embrace our type's way of being. This mindset can create immense pressure on both mothers and children for kids to conform to hard-and-fast expectations rather than allowing the natural development of each child's unique personality and gifts. As we will explore in depth in part 2, our core motivations—that is, our core fear, core desire, core weakness, and core longing—are the primary forces behind these parenting patterns and standards. Taking the time to explore each of the nine types' core motivations will help you gain a deeper perspective and understanding of the reasons you parent the way you do.

In the following descriptions of what each type generally wants to produce in their children, look for yourself in the tension of unmet expectations and the beauty of connection points, things you may have assumed were solely the result of your kids' good or bad behavior. Remember, none of these patterns are incorrect, bad, or shameful. They are merely the typical go-to patterns for each type. They can be both helpful and harmful, depending on a person's level of health in the moment. In part 2 of the book and at EnneagramForMoms.com, you will find more helpful insights and guidance in parenting well from your Enneagram type. But here are a few tangible ways we try to create our own type out of our kids.

What Each Type Is Trying to Create in Their Kids

1. **Type One moms are dedicated to raising "Little Principled Reformers"**—children who embody self-discipline, fairness, reliability, and the ability to make wise choices. These parents work hard to instill a strong sense of responsibility in their kids, guiding them to become little adults who are conscientious and uphold high moral principles. They emphasize the importance of self-control, reasoning, and the ability to delay instant gratification, and envision their kids as individuals who strive for excellence, maintain consistency, and make decisions based on what is right and just.

2. **Type Two moms are dedicated to raising "Little Nurturing Supporters"**—children who embody kindness, compassion, thoughtfulness, and attentiveness to others. These parents aim to nurture their kids to become little helpers, always eager to lend a hand and offer support to those in need (including their mom). They encourage their children to have a caring and giving nature, emphasizing the importance of being there for others and positively influencing their lives, and envision their kids as compassionate individuals who spread love and support, creating a nurturing environment for everyone they encounter.

3. **Type Three moms are dedicated to raising "Little Admirable Achievers"**—children who excel in various tasks, fulfill family ambitions, achieve their goals, and are physically attractive and popular. These parents inspire their kids to become little stars, radiating brilliance in every area of their lives, whether

it's academics, extracurricular interests, or social interactions. They encourage their children to strive for success, setting their sights on becoming role models and achieving recognition for their accomplishments, and envision their kids meeting very high standards.

4. **Type Four moms are dedicated to raising "Little Introspective Individualists"**—children who embrace their sensitive nature, explore their artistic abilities, delve into their emotions, and develop a profound understanding of themselves and others. These parents foster genuine empathy in their children to be kindhearted listeners who can truly connect with the emotions and needs of others. They inspire their children to delve into the depths of their inner world, express themselves authentically, and envision their kids using their individuality to bring vulnerability and beauty to the world.

5. **Type Five moms are dedicated to raising "Little Analytical Investigators"**—children who embody independence, curiosity, intellectual pursuit, and giftedness. These parents encourage their kids to become little geniuses, fostering their love for learning and empowering them to delve into the wonders of the world. They inspire their children to be inquisitive thinkers, always seeking new knowledge and exploring the vast realms of information, and envision their kids as self-reliant.

6. **Type Six moms are dedicated to raising "Little Faithful Guardians"**—children who embody reliability, obedience, resilience, and trustworthiness. These parents prioritize building a strong sense of loyalty and commitment in their children, teaching them to be steadfast supporters who remain by the side of their loved ones during challenging times. They help their kids learn to counteract the many uncertainties in the

world with extra due diligence and sometimes even wit or humor. They encourage their children to scan the horizon to be prepared for whatever comes their way and envision their kids staying safe and keeping others safe.

7. **Type Seven moms are dedicated to raising "Little Enthusiastic Optimists"**—children who exude energy, positivity, adaptability, and a willingness to embrace new experiences. These parents foster a love for trying new things and inspire their kids to be like young adventurers, spreading happiness and laughter wherever they go. They encourage their children to approach life with a zestful spirit and envision their kids always seeking out new opportunities for fun and exploration.

8. **Type Eight moms are dedicated to raising "Little Passionate Protectors"**—children who embody qualities of strength, independence, bravery, and resilience. These parents help their kids learn to stand up for themselves and to stand against injustice as they avoid being wrongly controlled or manipulated by others. They encourage their kids to develop a strong sense of self-assurance and determination, nurturing them to become young leaders, and envision their kids to fearlessly take on challenges and bring their ideas to fruition.

9. **Type Nine moms are dedicated to raising "Little Peaceful Accommodators"**—children who exhibit calmness, gentleness, empathy, compassion, and independence. These parents prioritize nurturing their children to become well-mannered, composed, and respectful. They help their kids learn to pay attention to more than one side of an issue, avoiding unnecessary conflict whenever possible. They encourage their kids to foster an environment of peace and kindness and envision their kids maintaining harmony for themselves and those around them.

Where did you see yourself in this list? Think of examples when your type shows up in your parenting. Your expectations and approaches are based upon very specific core motivations and strategies relevant to your Enneagram type. In part 2, you will be able to really delve into the intricacies of your type and how they affect your life as a parent. This will help you hone in on your true colors. Of course, remember that you can always flip over to part 2 anytime you want to. Maybe take a few moments to preview more ways your type is affecting your approach to parenting.

CHAPTER 6

Awakening to and Welcoming Our Thoughts, Feelings, and Inclinations

Let's face it: moments of stress or crisis can trigger our core fears and weaknesses, causing our internal world to spiral and produce external behaviors that contradict our parenting ideals. "We often try to control our children's feelings and behavior when actually it is our own internal experience that is triggering our upset feelings about their behavior."[4] In other words, we may believe the problem is our children's behavior when, in fact, it is our own reactiveness, impatience, or negative self-talk. When we eventually come to our senses, we may feel intense shame, guilt, or regret. Or worse, we may double down and justify our recent bad behavior by further blaming our children.

In our journey as parents (and in all our relationships), it's important to strive for emotional sobriety and self-regulation. We will more deeply explore concepts of self-regulation for our children in chapter 9. But if it all truly begins with us as moms, then we must learn to pursue an emotional state that allows us to respond to others out of love, joy, peace, patience, kindness, goodness, faithfulness, gentleness, and self-control. And in fact, we can learn to live in this state regardless of how our children or others may behave toward us. While it can be challenging and may appear daunting at times, such stability is a valuable objective to focus on as we consistently address our own inner world. This helps us understand how to treat others with love, empathy, and consideration, even when they are challenging or unwilling to meet us halfway. It's an ongoing process of self-discovery that leads to our own personal growth, which also nurtures a more supportive and compassionate environment for everyone else involved.

In moments when we are emotionally activated or caught up in our feelings, it can seem as if we are in an alternate state, functioning on emotional autopilot. What we need is to somehow become aware (in the moment) of our thoughts, feelings, and actions toward ourselves and our children so we can begin to understand why we behave the way we do. Understanding the reasons behind our behavior is the first crucial step before trying to fix the behavior. We must prioritize our hearts' emotional well-being before we can address our behaviors. But how can we become aware of these reasons when we don't even realize we are sleepwalking and repeating the same unhealthy patterns?

At Your Enneagram Coach, we have developed an incredibly helpful and easy resource that enables you to quickly wake up and become more familiar with your internal world. Our simple exercise is called A.W.A.R.E. It is a five-step application that will help you become conscious of what is happening in your inner world when you have unknowingly become emotionally activated and reactive. To help you get as much out of this tool as possible, I highly recommend dedicating a notebook as your Parenting Journal so you can write down your insights and come back to them as you continue on your path toward growth.

Below are the five steps that will eventually become natural for you to work through yourself:

AWAKEN to your thoughts, feelings, body sensations, and inclinations.

WELCOME these experiences without shame, criticism, or judgment.

ASK the parts of your heart what they are feeling and seek wise guidance.

RECEIVE what is true.

ENGAGE with yourself and your relationships in a new and healthier way.

I'm so excited to dive into this concept of becoming more self-aware. But as a fellow mom who understands the demands of busy and exhausting days, I imagine that you're seeking a few quick wins that will bring some practical relief. So for this chapter, let's just focus on the first two letters of AWARE, then we will explore the final three letters in the next chapter. Of course, the rest of the chapters will provide you even more tangible and straightforward tools to help you on your journey of self-discovery and growth, but for now, just know that I'm right here with you, cheering you on as you take one step at a time! Trust me, these early steps to becoming aware are huge milestones.

Awaken

The first step is to awaken to your thoughts, feelings, body sensations, and inclinations. We have already learned that our reactions are not solely the results of our kids' behaviors. More so, they are reflections of our greatest desires, dreams, or expectations for our children being unmet or misaligned in difficult or stressful moments. In the case of Nate chasing Libby, I wasn't awake to the ways Nate's specific behavior was clashing with my type's specific core motivations, which include my core fear of being in conflict, tension, or discord; feeling shut out and overlooked; or losing connection and relationship with others. In my moment of dysregulation, my core desire for inner stability and peace of mind was not being met.

Our bodies will usually inform us when we are misaligned in some way. It can be a headache, nausea, a surge of adrenaline in our stomach, tensing our fists or jaw, stress sweat, shutting down, dissociating, withdrawing, a dry mouth, or even something as comical as hurdling over a baby gate. A key element of waking up to what is happening before you unconsciously dive into actions or attitudes contrary to your own standards is to pay attention to these physical sensations, as well as to your thoughts and feelings. For me, somewhere in midair over the baby gate was the moment I woke up to feelings of anger, disappointment, control, and worry that were manifesting in my physical and emotional reactions.

Welcome

Once you've awakened to these thoughts and sensations and can name what you're feeling, you are free to do something most people have never done before: welcome these experiences without shame, criticism, or judgment. As we've discussed, mommy shaming is real and damaging, but it somehow seems valid to us in moments of internal crisis. Welcoming what you are experiencing without shame, criticism, or judgment can feel very foreign at first, but it is essential to peace and change. When we blow it with our kids, we are inclined to judge and resent ourselves, or to further heap our feelings of judgment and resentment upon our kids so we can rid ourselves of these thoughts altogether. Neither option brings true resolution.

How can we welcome these experiences that feel so steeped in shame? It begins with understanding that there is more than one thing going on inside you. Becoming aware begins with learning not to shame or hate whatever inner part of yourself has sent you spiraling.

And yes, I very intentionally used the language "whatever inner part of yourself" and not "whatever behavior from your kids" sent you spiraling. Our kids are not in charge of our reactions, so we must stop using them as excuses for our own negative reactions. Our response is still our responsibility.

Welcoming these experiences without shame is not the same as excusing them. We can and should acknowledge that we are fallen, imperfect people. But through God's love, we have been given grace. In the heat of your difficult parenting moments or shortly after the event, notice and welcome your body sensations, emotions, or unmet expectations. You don't have to fully understand them in that emotionally elevated moment. It is okay to take time to figure out and understand the workings of your inner world. Trust me, I know there isn't time for that when everything is crashing down. But instead of spiraling further, you can breathe and relax, knowing that God is with you. He embraces your weaknesses and mistakes with compassion and understanding. Because of his love for you, you can welcome and show kindness to yourself.

Taking small steps in this exercise will also help you become more ready to connect with your children, making them feel understood and supported in their struggles. Even though it might not seem like much at first, small steps toward awareness can lead to significant changes. Sometimes it takes a pivotal moment, a difficult situation, or simply the honesty of a trusted friend to help us start questioning our assumptions and move toward a more mindful way of living.

CHAPTER 7

The Rest of AWARE

As we are learning, awareness of our internal world is deeply connected to the idea that there is more than one thing going on inside us. I wrote much more about this concept in our previous book, *More Than Your Number*, and in other Your Enneagram Coach (YEC) resources at EnneagramForMoms.com. But as we move to the next step in our parenting journey of becoming AWARE, let's look a bit closer at the diversity of your own inner world so we will better understand what we mean by the next step of ASK.

In the last chapter, I used the term "parts" in discussing the different things that can be going on within us at once. My guess is that this term didn't seem odd to you, for good reason. In fact, the best way to explore your inner diversity is to think of yourself as having various internal parts. Just as you have an external family[5] who interacts with one another in varied positive and negative dynamics based upon any given situation, you also have a group of internal parts that interact with one another in much the same way.* We already use this language when we say things like, "Part of me doesn't want to be my kids' chauffeur, but another part of me wants my kids to be well-connected and well-rounded," or "Part of me doesn't want to cook tonight, but another part of me really wants to create a space for connection around our table." In reality, each of us use all nine Enneagram types to varying degrees, even though one reigns supreme: our main type. Therefore, these other types play a role within us. They are parts of us.

---

* In our previous book, *More Than Your Number*, we help you identify these parts in a model we created known as the Enneagram Internal Profile, or EIP.

As a mom, you might have one part that wants to be the perfect mom for your kids (Type One part), while another part feels deeply overprotective and tries to fix things for your kids (Type Two part). You might notice a part that wants your kids to be more courageous in seeking to succeed and be recognized by others (Type Three part). You may also have a part that worries your child won't fit in, concerned that a specific group may or may not accept them as their authentic self (Type Four part). You might notice a part that is trying to ensure your kids have all the facts and information they need to competently move forward in each situation they encounter (Type Five part). Perhaps one part wants to wrap your child in Bubble Wrap and keep them home where you know they'll be safe (Type Six part), while another part wants them to be adventurous and take more age-appropriate risks (Type Seven part). A strong and overprotective part wants to postpone dating so your kids don't experience sadness or betrayal (Type Eight part). Still another accommodating part wants to give in to your child's tantrums because you just need a little peace and quiet (Type Nine part). Can you see how there are many things going on inside you at the same time?**

Whatever your parts are doing, you can become attuned to how they show up in certain situations in healthy and unhealthy ways. To be clear, even though these other parts appear in our unique inner world, we never stop being our main Enneagram type with its core motivations. These other parts simply contribute their own shade to our unique personality's color, adding to the overall true colors of our internal makeup. Also, none of our parts are bad—in fact, they each desire to protect our main type, our truest self.

My main type is key because its core motivations are the driving force behind why I think, feel, and behave a certain way in any given circumstance. It can function in one of two ways: as the healthy and

---

** We go much deeper into the concept of our various internal parts in our previous book, *More Than Your Number*, which you can find by visiting EnneagramForMoms.com.

aligned Beloved Child or the unhealthy and misaligned Wounded Child.

I experience life as the Beloved Child when I am living aware of and trusting in how loved I am for who I am. I know that I don't have to be perfect to earn this love. I remember that I was made on purpose, with a purpose. I can rest in all that God wants for me, which means I can face life's ups and downs—including my life as a mom—from a mindset of wholeness. When I am living out of the healthy Beloved Child, my other inner parts also show up in positive and healthy ways, adding their strengths to the whole of me. Living as the Beloved Child doesn't necessarily secure a life of ease, but it does offer a joyful journey through the highs and lows rather than constantly reacting as I ride every emotional wave that comes.

However, in moments when I lose sight of my true status as the Beloved Child, I live as the Wounded Child. Some call this *spinning out*, *becoming activated*, or *getting triggered*. To be clear, healthily aligned people get triggered like anyone else, but they become aware and self-regulated enough that the implications are short-lived. They learn the process of observing it, acknowledging it, and allowing it to pass with healthy coping strategies. At times, all of us function from the inner place of the Wounded Child, becoming dysregulated or trying to control life on our own terms. In these moments of my own dysregulation, though I may still be aware of what's true, I respond to life differently. It is here that I stop living as one who is loved and secure. Instead, I become reactive, controlling, angry, irritable, critical, manipulative, dismissive, or isolated in a state of hiding.

This state of dysregulation causes my other parts to spin out as well. Suddenly, the unhealthy "shadow sides" of my parts start showing up, producing a lot of inner noise. Ultimately, these dysregulated parts are trying to help and protect my Wounded Child from its greatest fears. As counselors Dr. Alison Cook and Kimberly Miller theorize, it is as if these other inner parts are like scared kids trying to drive a school bus. They want to keep the bus on the road and everyone safe. However, the adult who should be driving, the Beloved Child, is asleep in the back seat.[6]

So how do we learn to self-regulate in these spun-out moments? We must wake up the Beloved Child by engaging in some sort of mindful process that helps us stop sleepwalking in anger, fear, or insecurity. This brings us back to the AWARE exercise. We have explored awakening to our thoughts, feelings, body sensations, and inclinations, and welcoming these experiences without judgment, criticism, and shame. We are now ready for the next three steps: ASK, RECEIVE, and ENGAGE.

> **AWAKEN** to your thoughts, feelings, body sensations, and inclinations.
>
> **WELCOME** these experiences without judgment, criticism, and shame.
>
> **ASK** the parts of your heart what they are feeling and seek wise guidance.
>
> **RECEIVE** what is true.
>
> **ENGAGE** with yourself and your relationships in a new and healthier way.

Ask

After you have welcomed your experiences, you need to ask these various parts of your heart what they are feeling.*** What are they trying

---

***   To gather more insights on how your most connected parts show up to help you, read about your Enneagram Internal Profile in chapter 28, or check out our book *More Than Your Number* at EnneagramForMoms.com.

to communicate, and more importantly, what are the motivations behind these thoughts and feelings? Is a certain negatively activated part connecting to a wounding story or a false internal message from your childhood? At this point in the exercise, resist the urge to fix your situation, and just let your internal parts—and their role in your story—simply be seen and heard.

When we welcome and extend kindness to these internal parts of ourselves without guilt or shame, we can become curious instead of critical. And believe it or not, developing curiosity is important for ourselves and our kids, even when we have to correct them. Siegel says, "Curiosity is the cornerstone of effective discipline."[7] This is equally as true for the self-discipline developed in our internal worlds as it is for the external discipline we use in interactions with our kids.

Before my infamously heated moment of Babygate, instead of hating or shaming myself, I could have stopped and welcomed with curiosity whatever dysregulated inner part of myself was freaking out. Could it be that Nate was not meeting my Type Nine expectations for keeping the peace and avoiding conflict? Maybe I was internalizing the fact that he was being mean to his sister, which was triggering my core fear that this might initiate a pattern of my children losing connection with each other, creating discord in our family over time? These kinds of questions are what I mean by being curious about what's going on inside your inner world.

Out of this curiosity, we learn that what starts as a thought or a reaction is actually connected to a deeper feeling—and that these feelings are connected to our internal story and our type's core motivations. We can stop acting as if our mistakes have negated our good intentions as parents and instead realize that whatever is causing these problems just needs to be redirected, reassured, and ultimately, reminded of the hope that redeems our ongoing stories.

The final part of the "ask" step is the most critical: ask for help to interpret what these parts are truly trying to say. Ask for guidance in what is true by listening and responding well to trusted guides. In many cases, if your story is especially painful or involves complex trauma, it is wise to also seek professional help. God uses many tools to work in our lives. Regardless, inviting God into all these spaces creates room for divine insight and intervention that we could never produce in ourselves.

Receive

Once we've listened to the story and messages our inner parts are believing or misbelieving, whether they're true or not, we can take the freeing step of embracing truth and living it out. It might feel like a repetitive process, but each time we accept forgiveness and compassion, letting truth guide our wounded and misaligned parts, we move closer to emotional stability. Therefore, take a few minutes to recall God's love for you and the inherent worth he has bestowed upon you, just as you are. Consider how your personality, especially in a healthy state, can bring blessings to others simply because you were created to be uniquely you. Replacing the lies that often bombard you with the truth will help slow down your inner turmoil and enable you to find your emotional balance again.

Engage

Finally, once we are beginning to believe truth instead of false messages, we are free to again face our external circumstance, engaging ourselves and our relationships in new and healthier ways. Now that we are more fully awake, we can see through the eyes of the Beloved Child, which allows us to reengage our children with curiosity, patience, humility, and authenticity—responding in the same ways

God engages with us. From this newly aligned place, our children experience the same unconditional love and acceptance we are learning to receive for ourselves.

Our kids will watch us grow in resilience through our own highs and the lows, and though they're most likely different types, they will see that we consider their type to be just as wonderful as our own. We won't be worried about clashing colors. Without parental perfection or control, we will be modeling self-awareness and self-regulation. Becoming aware allows us to fully attune to them, drawing out and appreciating their developing story in healthy ways. Since there is no shame, they begin to come into the wonder and fullness of their own unique personality expressed in their type.

By being willing to become aware of ourselves, we help our kids see themselves as God sees them: true gifts to the world. And when this pattern becomes a family practice over time, we make space for incredible new stories to be written, ones we may have never thought possible.

CHAPTER 8

Strange New Colors: Parallel Growth and Patient Curiosity

Becoming more aware of our inner world can help us better understand and attend to our children's emotions, leading us to become mindful of both our feelings and theirs. Recognizing the differences between the two helps us avoid trying to make our kids just like us or judging them for their differences. Instead, we can learn to embrace who they are becoming, regardless of how it relates to our ways of seeing the world.

Along the way, get ready to be surprised by more than just the changes you see in your kids as you support and love them toward maturity. As it turns out, our kids lead us toward change as well, especially when challenges push us outside our comfort zones so that we learn to depend on God's guidance. It's a humbling experience but also a beautiful one. In *How Children Raise Parents*, author and therapist Dr. Dan Allender points out that children are powerful catalysts for their parents' growth.[8] This means that the journey of parenting is more profound and change-inducing than most of us realize when we first have kids. This perspective invites us to embrace the surprising transformation that occurs within ourselves as we raise our children, recognizing that both parties are being shaped and molded in the process.

Your kid is changing you, and obviously they are still changing as well—but it is important to realize that their ongoing development is not solely a reflection of your parenting. Our children's growth is not all up to us—and this is great news, giving us permission to take a breath and pay attention to the other variables affecting their changing internal worlds. In this way, we bless both our kids and ourselves when we learn to walk not just ahead of them but also alongside them with curiosity and joy, nurturing the unique person God is creating them—and us—to be. This journey is challenging, unfolding like a daily revelation, bit by bit. In other words, when you walk with them in this way, you may see things in them that you never expected.

Remember how our kids are not cans of white paint but that certain colors reside within them that are yet to be revealed? Well, there's more to learn from this idea. If you order a certain shade of orange and watch the paint store technician add whatever the color code calls for to be poured into the white base, you will notice that some colors are added that are not orange. Yet, in the end, they all blend during the mixing process to become the shade they were intended to be. It seems impossible, right? How can a seemingly contrasting dash of silver or blue somehow be added to a whole that comes out as a shade of orange?

In the same way, as your children grow, you will sometimes see what seems like contrasting or confusing elements emerge, challenging what you thought you knew about their personalities. They may act a certain way that seems contrary to another way they've been acting. As their developmental seasons keep changing, so do they. And sometimes, they change back. With all this change, some clashing colors may show up—new attitudes, interests, or behaviors that seem counter to who you thought they were. Don't worry—all these will eventually mix to produce the unique personality they are supposed to have. There will be moments when you will swear that you know who they've become, including their type, but you may be seeing only a season in which a certain color is showing up brighter (or darker) than what will eventually be. As moms, we need to be patient and trust that it all won't fully make sense until their personality has been mixed over time by the experiences of their adolescence and life.

Having patience can be hard during these times. Since we cannot yet be fully aware of our kids' types, we often feel left in the dark about what is truly motivating them to certain attitudes and behaviors. Yes, we can pay attention to evidence about their internal wiring, but since we can't yet fully know, if we don't remain patient and curious, we can inadvertently misinterpret where their actions and emotions are truly coming from. For example, a Type Four kid whose personality has not yet been fully developed will often feel disconnected from and misunderstood by both of his parents because Fours harbor an inner belief that they are defective, flawed, misunderstood, and that they don't belong. But since his parents probably do not know that this is where his feelings are coming from, they may agonize and wonder what they did wrong.

It is good to highlight this example because parents in this specific situation might blame themselves for their child's feeling of disconnection, believing they did something to cause it. I want to help you understand that many parts of your child's personality are already hardwired in them from birth but don't begin emerging until later in life. Yet even early on, they naturally see, interpret, and react to their life with certain defensive mechanisms and strategies, conflict and communication styles, false internal messages, and so much more. While these may not be defined enough to determine their type just yet, they are there nonetheless, affecting the way they show up in the family. Again, moms do play a crucial role in passing along to their children a set of values, insights, relational boundaries, and more; but there are certain aspects of your child's personality that have nothing to do with what you have done or not done.

As I said before, in those tragic situations where parents are abusive or neglectful, a feeling of disconnection in a child is absolutely caused by parental actions and behaviors. But in healthier scenarios like the Type Four kid example, moms don't need to automatically feel it is their fault or that they are responsible for every single feeling or thought going on inside their kids. However, we do have the opportunity to be curious, ask good questions, and seek genuine understanding of what they are feeling. And when we have done inner work for our own personality type and have grown in our awareness of them and ourselves, we can also learn to gently redirect our kids onto a path that is healthier for everyone involved, including us.

Another example may help. Unlike a Type Four kid, a Type Nine kid feels (or desires to feel) connected to both their parents. A parent might feel they have done an amazing job in building this connection with their child—that they did something right for this to happen. But for Type Nine children, this is a default mode. Yes, a thoughtfully kind parent will enhance this connection and an aloof or contentious parent will complicate it. But overall, the Nine will always feel or try to feel as connected to their parents as possible, even if they have to lose or betray their own wants or needs in the process.

This is why it is vital for us as parents to take the time to learn more and understand the natural hardwiring of each of the nine personality types (more on this in chapter 12). Since our kids can behave as multiple types in childhood before their actual type is discovered, remaining open, curious, and emotionally grounded will enable us to lovingly engage them, even when strange colors seem to be emerging from their inner mix.

Understanding that they are responding according to an inner script only they can hear helps us avoid giving ourselves undue praise or shaming ourselves unnecessarily as if we are the only variable in their lives. It also equips us to show up in helpful ways instead of overly criticizing them out of our own sense of insecurity or stubbornness. We can instead acknowledge what can be observed in this particular moment that is happening within them and attempt to guide them toward truths that counteract any lies we detect they may be hearing from within. In this way, we can move humbly toward our children with a non-anxious, connected presence that remains curious about them.

The truth is, our kids need our non-anxious, connected presence more than they need our expertise. They don't expect us to be perfect. They know we'll make mistakes and misunderstand them. What they need and crave are parents who are open to learning, ready to admit their mistakes, and willing to grow themselves as they walk alongside them. When our children see our dedication to personal growth and our willingness to be vulnerable and transparent, they feel safe to grow with us. This is especially important as they navigate the tricky teenage years, filled with self-doubt and challenges. They long to be seen, patiently and lovingly attuned to, and guided on the road of personal growth that we are also walking. The more we can walk beside them on a path that they know we're humbly traveling ourselves, the more they'll trust us when we offer encouraging truth to counter the negative lies they may be hearing on the inside.

This is not to say that kids will live only in the unhealthy messages of their types but that these messages already reside on the bottom of their unmixed can of paint and often come out in ways that leave moms scratching their heads. Again, the temptation is to respond to the negative aspects of whatever activates our kids by aligning them with our own motivations. In essence, we say, "Your approach is all wrong. You should adopt my approach instead!" Since we want things to go well for our kids, we lean into what we perceive as the healthiest paths, the ones we have learned how to navigate ourselves over time. We know how much hurt and difficulty it took to get to where we are in adulthood, and we desire to help our kids avoid this pain by attempting to help them skip straight to where we are on our current paths. But we must remember that even though we walk beside them, we are still on two different paths—paths that just happen to be closely parallel to each other because we are sharing a family life together.

Of course, regardless of our personality types, there are many things we can share and guide our children into that will prove helpful. Teaching our kids to be kind, to resolve conflict with friends and family, or to practice good hygiene—these are lessons that all Enneagram types need to learn. However, each type will perceive them from their own unique perspective. Even if we can get our kids to mimic a certain behavior, we are still not necessarily parenting them according to their type's core motivations. A Nine's reasons for being kind are different from a Six's—one wants to keep the peace, while the other wants to be a loyal friend who can be depended on.

This is why it is important to pay attention to our own type's perspectives and reasons for relating to life's circumstances, never assuming or demanding that our kids show up in the world in the same way we do. Otherwise, we can find ourselves resisting and resenting the very things God has placed in our children that make them unique and beautiful. Instead, we can enjoy the waiting and watching with patience and curiosity.

CHAPTER 9

Premature Typing, Self-Regulation, and Long-Term Empathy

As we wait and watch, we will continue to see certain personality traits and behaviors emerge in our kids. This can naturally lead us to finally give in and guess what Enneagram type they may be. This is normal and reveals a healthy desire to understand and know our children, but at the same time, we should exercise caution in assigning a child a type too early.

Knowing a person's Enneagram type is all about why they think, feel, and behave based on their core motivations. Only the individual themselves can reveal the true inner workings of their heart. Since young children are still learning about themselves and the world around them, they will often not be able to know precisely why they think, feel, and behave a certain way on a core level. Therefore, we must remain patient while being curious, inquisitive, and observant until the day they are self-aware enough to confidently identify their main Enneagram type. Otherwise, we can begin parenting from a well-intentioned but still ill-informed or misinformed perspective.

Let me provide you with a few brief examples of why it's essential not to assign Enneagram types to our children prematurely, before they've had a chance to explore and discover their own type.

I was born a Type Nine, but others might not have been able to clearly see it in my early years. Like many Type Nines, known as Peaceful Accommodators, I spent a lot of my childhood watching and imitating the behavior of my parents and other adults. My goal was to make them happy and avoid conflict; so depending on the situation, I might have appeared to be a different personality type. Even though my parents didn't know about the Enneagram, my Type Seven dad and my Type Six mom may have assumed that I was more like each of them at different times because I easily adapted to their personality styles to maintain harmony. This meant that I showed up in different ways depending on the circumstances in order to make others happy and peaceful. Due to all the merging, blending, and adapting in my early years, it took a long time for me to discover my genuine self and type. This is common, especially for Type Nine children.

Can you see why it's important not to assign our kids a type too early in life? Doing so is simply the other side of the same coin of attempting to force kids to be our own color (see chapter 4). In the first case, we try to align our kids with our own personality types. In the second, we try to parent and shape them into whatever type we assume they are. But the result is the same in both cases: we ultimately fail to parent them according to their actual type—and most likely, we do so out of an unhealthy place within our own inner world.

For example, we may notice that our child is caring and helpful, so we assume they are a Type Two, the Nurturing Supporter. However, they may be kind and caring not because they are inwardly motivated to be helpful and appreciated like a Type Two, but because they are afraid of breaking the rules like a Type One. Or they may be this way because they want others to see that they are more caring than their peers out of some sense of competition or ambition for recognition, which is more indicative of a Type Three. Or they may behave out of a desire to provide and protect other people like a Type Eight. But if we are pleased with their behavior and assume they are whatever type best suits our expectations or needs for peace in the family, we may fail to remain curious about their evolving personalities and needs in the changing seasons to come.

We can clearly see that until a child's personality has time to fully emerge from real-life experiences so that they themselves can identify and confirm their own Enneagram type, we should avoid the mistake of confidently typing them and basing our parenting solely on this assumption. It is perfectly fine to hold several types loosely as possibilities and see which kind of nurturing or guidance seems to land on them best, but it is not wise to declare our kid to be a specific type. We should allow them to discover this for themselves and reveal it to us when they are ready.

I know how hard this is because this was the very journey I walked. I learned about the Enneagram when Nate was three years old and Libby was one. I desperately wanted to know and solidly land on their types. But as I look back, I am grateful that I remained curious rather than conclusive because my assumptions throughout the years panned out wrong, and they could have caused my kids undue emotional or developmental stress.

In *More Than Your Number*, I told the story of Rannulph Junuh, the main character in the movie *The Legend of Bagger Vance*, starring Matt Damon and Will Smith. A World War I veteran suffering from the ongoing trauma of seeing his entire company wiped out in battle, Junuh struggles with alcoholism and depression. Once a popular young man in Savannah, Georgia, he returns home during the Great Depression to help a friend by playing in her golf tournament as she attempts to restore her family's lost fortune.

As a pro golfer, Junuh's struggles continually clash with others' expectations of him. Everyone around him is freaking out with excitement and anticipation, desiring to see the athlete they love return to his earlier form. But their overwhelming, even anxious energy does not motivate him to do better. Instead, he internalizes it and begins to live out the anxiety he feels from everyone around him, producing even more pressure for him to come through for the town. This is what parents can inadvertently do to their children. Though well-meaning, parents often put pressure on their kids to come through for the family—to show up as a certain personality type that everyone expects and needs.

Again, as a Type Nine, the Peaceful Accommodator, I wanted to create little angels who were calm, peaceful, empathetic children. Type Eights, the Passionate Protectors, on the other hand, want their children to stand up for themselves so that no one can control them. Likewise, the citizens of Junuh's town wanted him to become who they wanted him to be so that their needs and expectations could be met. Up to that point, no one had tried to figure out what was actually happening within Junuh apart from the dynamics of everyone else around him.

No one, that is, until Bagger Vance shows up and becomes Junuh's caddy. Bagger Vance remains the only non-anxious, connected presence throughout the entire story. They meet as Junuh is hitting golf balls in the dark. Vance walks up right in front of him, remaining humorously calm and honest because he knows that with the way Junuh is playing, he could never hit a ball straight enough to hit him.

Throughout the story, Bagger Vance remains steadily present, never trying to fix Junuh. He always believes in him, is always willing to help. In times of stress, Junuh pushes back, but Vance never tries to force him into anything. Instead, he consistently points out the clear and best path for Junuh but leaves him to find it for himself in his own unique way.

Let's be careful here. For moms, there are some things we can't be passive about, things that will require a more adamant or protective approach. I'm not saying that we allow our kids to figure out right and wrong on their own, nor that we should not have very well-defined boundaries for their words, attitudes, and actions. Still, the principle rings true that when we freak out in reaction to our kids freaking out, we do not teach them not to freak out.

We can't know all the internal messages and motivations our kids are experiencing, but we can choose not to measure our reactions based solely on our own motivations or internal messages. We should most certainly redirect and correct our children, offering boundaries, structure, and discipline, but we can do so as one who is non-anxious in our response to their anxiousness, allowing whatever colors are within them to keep developing as we live life together with them. We can foster a safe and helpful relationship wherein they can keep making sense of their own story. Siegel and Hartzell write, "From the beginning of life, the mind attempts to make sense of the world and to regulate its internal emotional state through the relationship of the child with the parent. Parents help children regulate their internal states and bring meaning to experience."[9] So while our role as "mom" doesn't solely determine the kind of personality that develops within them, we are still vital to helping them learn how to practice healthy emotional self-regulation, regardless of what type they ultimately are.

But like Bagger Vance with Junuh, helping your kids self-regulate is based more on presence and empathy than pressure or control. Proximity with patience makes all the difference. But how do we maintain a non-anxious, connected presence ourselves when our kids are anything but non-anxious? This is the heart of the matter, isn't it? As much as we can't ask our kids to show up in ways foreign to their unique makeup, we also can't simply decide to show up as a non-anxious, connected presence without doing the work of regulation for our own internal state. As we have already learned and researcher Dr. Curt Thompson attests, a parent's capacity to be aware of their child's developing mind and emotions is directly and deeply related to whether they themselves have first made sense of their own developmental story.[10] If we are spun out, they, too, will be spun out.

This means we must go beyond seeing the AWARE exercise as a one-time nicety to file away. No, we must become long-term students not just of our kids but also of our own inner worlds. As a mom, if I can learn to become aware of my own personality perspective and story as a consistent pattern of being, then I will be able to hear my kids more clearly, responding to their true selves and experiences for what they are, without "pouring my paint" all over them by forcing them to be as I am and see the world as I do. Our work continues because awareness over time matures into attunement. Our goal is to attune to our kids with our patient presence so we can come alongside them as a regular practice, guiding them in the way they should go, not controlling them from above.

Again, instead of trying to type them too early or hurry through a certain problem, attuning to what our kids are feeling allows us to show up in a non-anxious, connected, and empathetic way. "Empathy is our parenting superpower," writes author and researcher Hunter Clarke-Fields. "It's the skill that will help our children achieve the holy grail of their own emotional regulation. When we can sense what our children are feeling and experiencing—and be present with them—we are building connection and attunement." But again, I can't just attune to my kids without first attuning to my own story as a regular practice I engage in without judgment. Clarke-Fields continues, "Note that offering empathy requires that our own cup is full. Making self-care a priority is vital to being able to offer kindness and empathy."[11]

This is not about fixing ourselves so we can fix our kids. Rather, it means remaining curious about the way God has created us, knowing that he doesn't make mistakes. I want to honor his lovingly creative work in me by better knowing myself. In this place over time, I become more like the person he has created me to be, not the way other people say I should be.

Mom, no matter how hard it gets, we can keep learning to regulate ourselves, even when life's circumstances threaten to overwhelm us. As we walk this journey, our kids receive something important from our self-regulation. Their ability to regulate themselves can only happen if we become aware of our own internal disorganization in any given moment of crisis—and yes, this takes practice. But if becoming aware of why our emotions have been activated becomes second nature, then we will be more able to make room for our kids to do the same.

CHAPTER 10

Messy Kitchens and
False Messages

After several years of our family becoming more aware of our internal worlds, a big revelation took me by surprise. When Nate and Libby were older—seventeen and fifteen, respectively—it wasn't unusual for me to spend long hours upstairs in my office, working hard on building the content and community for what would eventually become Your Enneagram Coach. One summer morning, I came downstairs to find the kids awake, enjoying a well-deserved break from school. They were having a great time playing video games together in front of the TV. I was thankful that they were not just siblings but also friends who usually got along with each other. Video games on a hot summer day was their plan, and their laughter filled our home with warmth and happiness. It was truly heartwarming to witness their bond grow.

But something else also caught my attention: the mess they had left behind in the kitchen. It looked like a storm had come through! I'm sure you can relate. I had used only one dish that morning, so it was clear who the culprits were. I decided to do what any mom would do: I told them I was going back upstairs to work for a while and asked if they would tidy up the kitchen before I returned in a couple of hours. They agreed without any fuss. "Sure, Mom! No problem!" With the stress of my workday, it was a relief to know they were going to take care of it.

My time upstairs stretched longer than I'd planned. About four hours later, I headed back downstairs and there they were, still engrossed in their video games. And there it was, the kitchen looking just as chaotic as before. They had done nothing.

At that moment, my feelings were all over the place. Different parts of me had various reactions to what I was seeing. One part was grateful; I mean, they were having fun and getting along, which was something I always aimed for as a mom. Especially as a Type Nine, creating a peaceful atmosphere in our home is a big desire, and right then, it was happening. But then another part of me started to kick in at full throttle, and not in a good way. Every mom can probably relate to being activated here, each with her own reasons based on her core motivations and her own story. For me, the kids had pressed a major button of my Type Nine personality, sending my internal alarms blaring.

Each Enneagram type carries its own set of false messages. (More information on each type's false messages in part 2.) These messages run in the background like a playlist in our minds that never stops. They are thoughts that we automatically jump to, and they stir up all sorts of reactions inside us. Often, something external cranks up the volume of these messages, tempting us to believe that others are intentionally sending us certain negative messages. As a Type Nine, I've got my own familiar playlist of these messages always humming in the background. *You're not important to others. Your voice doesn't matter. You're never good enough. Nobody really wants you.*

When I saw that messy kitchen, my familiar internal false messages suddenly became louder, trying to convince me that my kids were intentionally communicating these hurtful things to me through their actions. It happens so fast that we often don't realize we're making pretty big assumptions about others' unspoken intentions. The result is that our feelings, thoughts, and even physical sensations all start buzzing, creating a mix of not-so-great emotions and unhelpful reactions.

At one point in my life, this pattern was my norm. Let's flash back to when Nate and Libby were much younger, before I began better understanding the true colors of my internal world through the insights of my Enneagram type. In those days, when I said something to them and they didn't listen, I instinctively thought they were intentionally disobeying or disrespecting me. Even though they were so young, my Wounded Child began to hear and believe these familiar false messages as if my little kids were somehow intending to hurt me in the specific ways that so easily wound my heart. My Wounded Child would often go into fight, flight, freeze, or fawn (people-pleasing) mode to safeguard itself from perceived threats.

But by this point in my life, armed with more knowledge about my own story and personality, I felt better equipped to identify what was actually happening within me. I had discovered that I could awaken to my feelings when I first became activated, verify whether my assumptions were accurate by welcoming them and asking my inner parts, receive truth as truer than whatever perception was spinning me out, and then engage more healthily by choosing a more emotionally balanced reaction based on reality rather than assumption. It is like driving and noticing your car beginning to drift onto the shoulder of the road. Newfound awareness and understanding are like rumble strips on the side of the highway, alerting you when you begin to veer off the road. Once you hear the rumble, you can either decide to make a healthy course correction or to keep going the same destructive way.

On this day, I could hear the rumble and I sensed that I was entering the kitchen in a triggered state. Remember: getting triggered isn't wrong! It's just a part of life. We all face moments when misplaced feelings, unproductive thoughts, and false assumptions become really loud within us. But when we become angry, it doesn't mean we have to react in ways that are harmful and unhelpful to the situation. We can avoid misguided reactions without treating our feelings as if they are bad in themselves. It is important to recognize that these initial strong feelings become naturally activated and usually can't be avoided, nor should they be.

Once we are activated inside, what truly matters is how we work through the steps toward a different engagement. In emotionally charged situations, do we take time and pause and become AWARE? Do we ask clarifying questions before just spouting off? I'll be honest with you, when I saw the state of the kitchen still in disarray, I wanted to get big and communicate exactly how upset, hurt, and disrespected I felt. The wounded part of my heart wanted to accuse, judge, and punish—basically do all the things that parents typically do to their teenagers when they are negatively activated by their actions. These are things I had done before, and returning to them felt easy and familiar.

Thankfully, since there was more than one thing happening within me, I was able to hear my Beloved Child, the one that could lead my wounded parts back to a healthier way of being and of interacting with my kids. This part of me knows that God has given me the ability to become more self-aware of what is happening within me and to take time to self-regulate instead of reacting impulsively. It was from this place that I was also able to remain patiently curious about the situation instead of becoming accusatory, since, at that point, all I had are my assumptions versus unknown facts.*

Rather than immediately resorting to yelling, which I had done in the past, I made an effort to acknowledge and welcome my thoughts, perceptions, assumptions, and feelings. I aimed to remain emotionally composed while asking curious questions to uncover the truth. Even so, what came out as I spoke to my kids was still a blend of sadness and frustration, just more controlled. "Hey, guys, what happened? I asked you to clean the kitchen before I came back downstairs and you agreed. Can you help me understand? Because right now, I feel activated inside. But before I jump to conclusions, I'd appreciate it if you could explain."

---

* You can learn so much more about the Wounded and Beloved Child in our book *More Than Your Number: A Christ-Centered Enneagram Approach to Becoming A.W.A.R.E. of Your Internal World* (Thomas Nelson, 2022).

What happened next was a surprise. As you'll discover, when you raise your kids with tools to enhance their emotional intelligence, be prepared for them to use those tools when interacting with you. Their response was quite different from what my Wounded Child had perceived and expected—and it still brings a smile to my face. I don't remember their exact words, but the sentiment went something like, "Mom, we got carried away playing games and having fun, and we just lost track of time. But we can understand how you, as a Type Nine, might feel disregarded and unheard. We didn't mean to make you feel like your presence and wishes don't matter. That's not how we see you because you matter a lot to us. We're genuinely sorry and we'll clean it up right now." Again, these weren't their precise words, but pretty close. I was taken aback. It meant a lot that they comprehended how a Type Nine tends to internalize certain false messages. They empathized with me in the moment, conveying truth that resonated with the way my heart is uniquely made.

This was the moment I realized that the inner work I'd been doing and modeling to my kids over the years was beginning to yield results. They were able to see through the tint of my Type Nine lens and to also communicate their own reasoning, emotions, and perspective.

Wherever you are in your motherhood journey, I share this story to inspire hope that every family member, including yourself, can indeed grow and change. Mom, don't lose hope, because progress is possible, which means there is purpose in consistently and humbly moving forward to set the example of emotional health. And even when we mess up, there is grace to try again and again. You'll need this grace, so don't be afraid to take it.

I want to be clear: not every interaction with my kids after this moment was transformed into something from a fairy tale or therapy book. The McCord family definitely still has its moments when things go awry. But moments like these offer me hope, making me deeply grateful to God. His truths and the insights from the Enneagram really did help my kids connect with their own inner worlds—and with mine. Sidestepping the usual unpredictable teenage responses of blame-shifting or excuse-making, they had learned to respond with understanding, compassion, and empathy. As we'll learn in an upcoming section, they met me halfway, engaging in acknowledgment, taking responsibility, apologizing, reconciling, and repairing.

If it happened for me, it can happen for you too.

CHAPTER 11

Choosing Relational Connection over Behavioral Control

I bet you've been where I was in the darker moment of my kitchen story. Maybe as a Type Two mom, you have felt rejected when your son didn't listen to your sound advice about creating the perfect volcano for the science fair. You believe that he didn't appreciate your help. Maybe as a Type Six mom, you have felt triggered over your daughter's simple, normal relationship problem with a friend. You believe that you aren't teaching her well to secure the safety of friendships in life.

It is natural to initially react to our kids' behaviors by assuming the worst messages we hear within us are truly being spoken through others' words or actions. And yes, when you peel back the layers of any given incident, sometimes the worst does prove to be true. Sometimes our kids just want to rebel and hurt us. Since they are human, they are more than capable of responding out of impure motives. But even when our kids are out to hurt us, we can still learn to manage our thoughts, emotions, and reactions.

Any given day, when I first become activated by someone else, it feels like I can see only their behavior. It is like an emotional eclipse. And it is tempting to stop there and stay in the shadows of focusing only on their behavior rather than my own internal messages. In referencing the work of author Alfie Kohn, Dr. Becky Kennedy says, "The behavior is only what's on the surface; what matters is the person who does the behaving . . . and why she does so."[12] If I had not taken a moment to at least attempt to awaken to the "why" of what was going on, I would've missed the opportunity to really hear and honor my kids' stories in that moment—and to have my own story also heard and honored. Had I come in hot as my wounded parts wanted me to—screaming, accusing, name-calling, and criticizing—my kids would've been much more resistant and reactive. Ironically, I would have invested in the very responses I least wanted to receive, which would have only sent me spiraling deeper into my own angry, dismissive attitude. I would have invited my worst fears and suspicions to come true.

Why do we so often react in these negative ways? It is because our inner selves tend to reflexively respond to situations according to these false inner scripts and messages. Author Hunter Clarke-Fields says, "We aren't 'choosing' to turn on our frustrated thoughts, helpless feelings, or physiological stress reaction. We react in those moments on automatic pilot. Our stress is running the show, dictating our reaction. Our words just fly out. Often, our autopilot script is a replay of the same language our own parents used in those situations."[13] Until we awaken to these inner messages, we stay stuck on emotional autopilot.

No one is exempt here. We all hear inward false and painful scripts and messages specific to our Enneagram type. Though we sometimes give in and act out these scripts, momentarily believing they are true, we can also recognize when we are being triggered and lean into the reasons why. This kind of awareness equips us to avoid the trap of reacting on chaotic autopilot.

One key here is to try to choose connection over control. Learning to value relational connection over behavioral control can keep us from jumping to incorrect assumptions that damage our relationships. Instead, this approach fosters conversation and leads to greater empathy from everyone involved. It accesses the advantage of knowing our own emotional stories and practicing our own self-regulation before we delve into our kids'. In the kitchen story, I was able to attempt to connect with my kids through a genuine and more curious tone before jumping straight to trying to aggressively exert control over their actions. In this case, my children were familiar with my core motivations and false messages. This familiarity gave them the space to be more self-aware, understanding, and compassionate. They were even able to self-regulate their emotional responses when being caught in a mistake that had turned into a conflict. These kinds of situations are when we most need self-regulation, and when we least want to access it.

Since Nate and Libby were nearly adults and aware of their own Enneagram types, I could also empathize with them based on their unique ways of viewing the world. Mom, when you feel triggered by your kids, it's vital to pause and try to understand their perspective. Why might they have seen or reacted to the situation differently than you? It helps to ask clarifying questions so you don't make assumptions that are inaccurate and harmful. This is living out what we've been discussing: the realization that our personality's outlook isn't the same as everyone else's. This awareness allows us to stay curious and open to other viewpoints, even when those viewpoints challenge our own assumptions connected to internal messages or past wounds.

If your children are younger and have not yet self-identified their main type, you can at least recognize that they are most likely not seeing the circumstance from your perspective. Try to remain curious so you can understand how they are interpreting the same circumstance through a different lens—one that you can't yet fully identify.

We exercise curiosity because we're wisely aware of our own lenses. Instead of only doubting the accuracy of the way others are seeing a situation, we learn to doubt the accuracy of our own perceptions as well. Not everyone will see things the way we do, and neither will everything land on their hearts as it does on ours. We must accept these realities rather than fight against them.

Stepping back is key. Instead of quickly assigning ill motives, stepping back gives us a chance to breathe and better share our emotions in a regulated manner. Otherwise, we can spiral around the room like a punctured can of spray paint. Siegel and Hartzell agree: "It is through the sharing of emotions that we build connections with others. Communication that involves an awareness of our own emotions, an ability to respectfully share our emotions, and an empathic understanding of our children's emotions lays a foundation that supports the building of lifelong relationships with our children."[14] Taking time to breathe allows us a better chance to share emotions rather than spew them—to understand instead of only seeking to be understood.

If you're worried about this approach, know that none of this means we should avoid giving consequences to our kids. Curiosity does not get them off the hook. We can show up with curiosity and they can respond with empathy and maturity—and we can still feel the need to require something of them that helps them learn, or helps the family as a whole. Nate and Libby really had made a mistake. For all they knew, I may have needed them to listen because we were having guests over later in the day and I needed their help to clean up. I could have thanked them for their empathetic responses and felt thankful for our good relationship, yet still have told them they were grounded from their video games.

There will always be ramifications of our kids' actions, as well as training or discipline that is needed after the fact. But how can we correctly train, guide, provide for, and support our kids in their own development if we don't fully understand the motives or reasons informing the situations we share? If we don't remain more curious than critical, we probably can't. In fact, if we haven't learned to be curious about the tones and shades of our own internal world, being curious about our kids' will feel foreign at best. At worst, we will be ill-informed in our attempts to discern what's going on within them, having not engaged in the same work within ourselves. Once again, the best indicator of their emotional health is our own. As Dr. Kennedy says, "Empathy comes from our ability to be curious: it allows us to explore our child's emotional experience from a place of learning, not judgment."[15]

Remember, our kids' actions and attitudes can indirectly turn up the volume of our inner false messages. But the truth is, children and teens are generally not yet equipped to pinpoint the nuances of these messages. They are usually too lost in their own thoughts, emotions, and life circumstances. Even when we feel activated, we can still connect with them as humans whom we love—and in doing so, we create room for more fruitful and peaceful outcomes for everyone involved, including ourselves. This also means honoring their personality types as being just as valuable as our own.

CHAPTER 12

If I Can't Know Their Types, What Do I Do?

God created me to be a Type Nine, while my son, Nate, is a Type Six, and my daughter, Libby, is a Type Two. We each have certain values we hold higher than others, based upon our types. As a Faithful Guardian, Nate will more deeply value safety, security, and loyalty in his relationships. As a Nurturing Supporter, Libby will value relationships, connection, and helping others. I, on the other hand, will more deeply value avoiding conflict, keeping peace, and being a nonjudgmental and receptive presence. None of these is better than the others. We each bring a different color to the divine palette God uses to paint our family's portrait.

Of course, when Nate was young, I didn't know he was a Six. I was pretty convinced he was either a One or a Two. And I couldn't tell if Libby was a Nine (like me) or a Two, but thankfully I never tried to settle on one type or the other. As we said before, when kids are young, we can't fully know their types. So when it comes to the Enneagram, there is one huge question from parents that is worth addressing again. *If I can't figure out my child's type, how can I show up in ways that bring calmness and strength to my kid—besides being healthy in my own type—as he struggles with the emergence of his own unknown personality traits?*

The answer is simple: become familiar with all nine types so you can equally value them. Again, part 2 will give you examples of the kinds of truth-filled, reassuring, gospel-informed messages the wounded parts of each type need to hear the most. As a mom, become an encourager-times-nine, speaking the reassurances and truths not only of your own type, nor only of whatever type you may suspect your kid is at present. Access the encouraging messages of all nine types.

Even though we each resonate with our main type and certain internal parts more than others, the truth is, each of us uses all nine types to varying degrees. This is why the emotional truths of each specific type are still helpful for all types. Your child may or may not be a Type One, but it is still encouraging and formative for her to hear and believe that "you are good." Even though they may or may not feel like they need to be perfect for themselves and others, you can help them see that striving for perfection is a never-ending pursuit that is impossible to achieve. Real perfection belongs only to God, and in relationship with him, our need for perfection has already been met. Likewise, your child may not be a Type Eight, but it will encourage their soul to hear and believe "you will not be betrayed." They may or may not feel that they must protect themselves against powerlessness and betrayal by having an invincible exterior, but God says he will protect them and never forsake them. Therefore, they are free to reveal their vulnerable heart with tenderness and patience. To some degree, all the truth messages will be helpful for all types to hear.

As a Nine, I do want to impart to my kids some of the strong and healthy attributes that naturally overflow out of me. There is nothing wrong with this, as long as I keep remembering to avoid trying to make them into mini-versions of myself. In this way, I engage in a twofold honoring of who I am as the mother God has put into their lives and who they will ultimately become as individuals. God is the Master Artist, but I get to be a part of all of it!

If moms don't equally honor both personalities—their own and their kids'—they will be prone to judge, criticize, blame, and punish them based on what they have experienced through their own personality's paradigm. They will engage with little understanding of what's happening from their kids' perspective, which is super confusing and shaming, producing undue guilt in their children. It also breaks relational bonds and connection because the children don't feel seen and understood.

We have discussed all of these, but there is an additional danger that follows: kids internalizing their parents' criticisms. They can begin to believe, *If that's what they say about me, I must be a horrible kid.* This is detrimental for any child to hear, but these kinds of internal messages will resonate even deeper in children who are certain types. This is why we must be careful not to project onto our kids messages that make sense to us as if they will automatically make sense to them. Both perspectives need to be balanced and honored.

Finally, if we don't pause and consider with curiosity what is happening within our kids, what are we actually punishing? We might think we're punishing our kids for being disrespectful by not doing the dishes, but that may not be the case. There may be more to be unpacked and understood. In this healthier approach, we may still give them consequences, but we will arrive at these consequences in the very different light of a fuller, compassionate, empathetic understanding.

I understand that not knowing your kid's type makes all this complicated. I get it. I started using the Enneagram when my kids were very young. I longed to know their types and have an exact instruction manual for each of them, but God does not set it up that way. He allows our kids' types to remain a mystery for quite some time so that we will remain dependent on his provision and care. This can be challenging, but I once again encourage you to be patient, while at the same time curious.

There will be moments in your child's life when you will swear that you know what type they are. Then suddenly, a shift in age or circumstance that moves them to be healthier or unhealthier will change everything you think you know. This is why it is unfair to them to put a stamp on it too early and to proclaim beyond a shadow of a doubt that any adolescent is a certain type. During these years, kids are simply not self-aware enough to know or articulate their true core motivation, which guides them to their main type.

As we remain curious, it can be interesting and even helpful to pay attention to the clues. You can hold several types loosely as you become a student of all nine types, which will ultimately prove to be the best way to grow as a student of your own child.

CHAPTER 13

Choosing Strengths over Negativity Bias

As we study our children, our attention is more easily drawn to certain things. Research shows that it is easier to identify what is wrong with others than what is right. Hunter Clarke-Fields explains, "We also don't consciously choose to focus on the problems. Because of [our] wiring for survival, we all have an innate propensity to be aware of things that could threaten—a negativity bias."[16] In other words, we are more likely to interpret what we see in a negative light than a positive one.

As your kid's personality type continues to blend and change through God's work in their life experiences, committing yourself to this deeper understanding of all nine personality types will help you better interpret what you are—and are not—seeing in them. In particular, you will be able to avoid a negativity bias toward them, which would lead to seeing only what they are seemingly doing wrong because it appears wrong through the single lens of your own type.* Otherwise, how do you even know what you're seeing?

For example, let's say that your child ultimately turns out to be a Type Eight. In childhood, this means they will most likely present as very assertive, strong, and direct. These are amazing, wonderful qualities for any adult to have when they are regulated and live them out in healthy ways. But especially if your little Eight is a girl, society will typically label her in a single way: a strong-willed kid who talks back a lot. What they can't see, but you may need to make room for, is that what appears to you, her teachers, and other family members to

---

* You will find more specific insight about how each type processes biases in part 2.

be "talking back" is actually immature expressions of her type's strong and curious dialogue. Everyone may also not be able to see right now that one day in her adult life, these traits will be evident strengths.

If we're not careful, we can ascribe a negative bias to something that is actually a positive strength. This can make the child feel that one of their greatest gifts is actually a weakness, which can cause them to live their lives shamefully repressed, frustrated, or unnecessarily at war with themselves. Instead of assuming a negative bias, a better path is to point out the positive as we redirect them to more mature expressions without shame.

Once when Nate was quite young, he disagreed with something his dad asked of him. In the moment, Nate bowed up his chest and offered a strong and seemingly defiant "No!" As Jeff is a Type Six, Nate's behavior could have been easily interpreted by Jeff as disloyal or disrespectful. However, Jeff chose a path of self-regulation instead. He gently sat him down and told him that there would be times in life when having such a strong "no" would be important, especially when defending the weak or taking a stand for what's right. However, he explained, such a "no" was not best used on his dad in this situation. He obviously tailored the talk to be age-appropriate, but instead of vilifying Nate's expression, he helped him to see how most things in our lives can be used for either good or bad pursuits. He helped him not to categorize one of his strengths as only a weakness, but rather as something to be understood, managed, and accessed in appropriate ways.

As parents, whenever it is possible, we must try to find and affirm the good in our kids' difficult moments, even if the only thing we can find seems small or insignificant. It usually is neither. Affirming the positive helps us bring a fuller perspective to both their understanding and ours, rather than simply shutting everything down that doesn't naturally resonate with a mature expression of our own type or values. I fear that many beautiful, yet underdeveloped shades within kids are often branded as ugly because parents or culture want to add a label instead of seeing what good can be acknowledged and redirected, even if consequences are still necessary.

A Type Five child needs time to emotionally recharge, but many parents (especially highly extroverted parents) can become very frustrated by this, thinking that their kid just wants to isolate from the family. Curiosity and connection seek, without shame, to find what positives may not yet be fully evident in their lives. In the case of a Type Five (and for all children), our willingness to cultivate space, time, or energy for them when they obviously need it actually protects and empowers them. Instead of assuming that their need to be alone is always negative, we can choose to see the creativity and the sense of wonder about the world that Fives dive into when are by themselves.

Our kids' strengths may not always look like strengths to us, so we must become aware of our tendency to approach them from a place of scarcity and unawareness. As Hunter Clarke-Fields explains, your "negativity bias can undermine your connection to your child—a.k.a. the glue that makes parenting easier. We see our kids' uncooperative moments—how about the cooperative ones? We see their selfishness—maybe missing their generosity. Our view of our children can become narrow and biased."[17]

This is why we must strive to remain curious, emotionally sober, calm, and patient with a non-anxious, connected presence, knowing that we're not yet seeing the full color of what they will bring to the family portrait. Pointing out the positive keeps us from seeing through a darkened lens that robs our kids—and ourselves—of the joys of their adolescent journey.

CHAPTER 14

Grace for Supermoms

Early on, we talked about the idea of supermoms. Hopefully, our journey since then has helped you view your life with a fresh sense of hope that doesn't hinge on how well you perform as a mom. But how do we truly embrace this way of being as a long-term way of living? It begins with remaining mindful of our real and present need for grace. This will also require us to establish new habits that help us return to this grace day after day. In the stress and madness of everyday parenting, this false idea that you should be a supermom is one of the main challenges that makes it difficult to keep coming back to this place of receiving daily grace. The cape just gets in the way.

If you're like me, there are moments when you've wished you could achieve this supermom status, striving to meet an ideal image of what it seems a great mom should be. These desires come from a good place in your heart, but they can quickly lead into a harmful cycle of striving, comparing, judging, condemning, and shaming yourself and others. When we compare, we either lift ourselves up by putting others down, or we lift others up by putting ourselves down. Either way, we're putting someone down. On the other hand, a better way that comes from a higher truth leads us to encourage one another and to build one another up. This means learning not to participate in comparison or the shaming of other moms or ourselves.

Although the term "supermom" was originally intended as a compliment to honor mothers for their hard work and dedication, it has also unintentionally set up unrealistic expectations in our culture, which is why some now see it as a negative label. It reinforces the mistaken notion that we should be flawlessly capable in every area of life. It also undermines the truth that parenting is a shared responsibility among partners and a supportive community. Moms can begin to believe the false idea that asking for help or taking breaks signifies weakness. This misconception has detrimental effects on both moms and their families.

When society expects mothers to be "super," we undervalue the beauty of just being—that is, being our true selves and being fully present with our children. What do we know about Supergirl? She's rarely present because she's always flying to fix everyone else's problems. While helping others is inspiring and often necessary, Supergirl does not have a very balanced life. She's split between a superhero and a woman hiding her identity behind glasses because she can't allow her true self to be known. Throughout any superhero narrative, you will find that the hero is desperate for a break, longs to find comfort in a genuine community, and wants to be fully known and understood. That's no way to parent.

You don't need to be a supermom; just being a mom is enough. You are enough. Instead of labeling each other as supermoms, let's acknowledge and appreciate all our hard work while also recognizing our need for balance, self-care, outside support, and a realistic approach to parenting. When I feel as if I have to measure up to a certain image, it becomes much more difficult to avail myself of the grace extended to me in every single moment of my parenting journey—including the ugly ones. To become healthier, I have to examine the lenses that are coloring my supermom expectations.

Take a moment to process this for yourself: Who is the supermom you see in your head? Where does she come from? Perhaps she is a combination of your childhood impressions and experiences, or maybe the impossibly high (and imaginary) bar set by perfectly filtered social media moms you see on your phone. Or maybe you have friends or church leaders who regularly point out a particular image that you must become in order to reach what they consider to be the ideal mom status.

The thing is, just knowing that supermom doesn't actually exist is not enough to silence the unending feeling of critique, scarcity, and comparison most moms feel over her. Our problem is not purely cognitive or facts-based. It goes much deeper into the false messages being believed by our main type and our other internal parts. These parts need more than to be merely educated; they need to be comforted and restored to a right sense of identity in grace.

As you already know from your own experiences, our false messages can be loud and convincing. For me, it used to feel like I needed to mirror the moms that everyone saw as esteemed in our church, on social media, and on YouTube. Chasing these other moms' ever-evolving rules meant that, for me, the scenery was always changing in confusing and disappointing ways. And even when I did identify and adhere to some of their insights, my kids' stages of life were always changing, so the rules suddenly wouldn't work in the new season or with my family's varying personalities. Trying to paint by someone else's numbers just made a big mess of my family portrait.

Comparison only made me feel miserable. Yet, I instinctively felt I could still somehow become a supermom because these sources encouragingly told me that I *could*, which also made me feel like I *should*. I was wrong on both counts—and the influencers weren't the real problem. They meant well and usually offered helpful tips and suggestions. The problem was that their external messages resonated with negative messages I was already hearing on the inside. No matter what they were actually saying, what I heard from these women reinforced the false belief that if I would just follow someone else's prescriptions, doing more and more work to foster a perfect childhood environment for my kids, "supermomhood" (along with "super kids") could actually be attained. I allowed my mind to believe that I was seeing and hearing from supermoms who were actually attaining it.

The truth is, neither we nor the influencers will ever become the elusive ideal we chase after. Believing in this notion will leave you feeling as I did: like a failure, always falling short, and constantly thinking you're failing your kids. Was I perfect? No, but these extreme viewpoints of myself were not the full truth either. These perspectives lacked grace and kindness, and they didn't help me answer the question, *Who is the mom God has uniquely designed me to be for the specific children he has entrusted me to raise?*

You've heard the story already, but Jeff helped me see the super-mom standard I was chasing after for what it truly was: a mirage. I began facing the lies that were stealing the joy of motherhood from moments that were deeply meaningful. Slowly, I started believing that every mom has her own struggles, even if she doesn't necessarily display them on social media or on the playground.

Beyond all this, I began to envision myself leaving these comparisons behind altogether, even if they were leading me to see that others were struggling as I was. Even if this were true, what did it matter? All that I am created to do is to live out my relationship with my own children, based on how we're uniquely made and within our own circumstances.

This wasn't merely an aha moment of finally figuring things out through information gathering. I needed more than facts. I needed comfort, direction, and the embrace of Someone who truly comprehended my inner world. I needed an Author and Perfecter of my faith story, one who was writing it and who promised to see it through to its perfect end.[18] I met Someone who is always there to enter my inner world with gentleness, empathy, and genuine strength. All the strategies I thought I should pursue had to eventually yield to my authentic self: my identity in Christ and the unique way he has created me. This involved recognizing all the external pressures to measure up, along with the false ideals I carried within. I had the most remarkable revelation: Christ stands as the ultimate superhero, fully redeeming me and continually caring for me and our family.

Even though my kids are adults now and I've come a long way, I still wrestle with the false messages. I'm a mom through and through, so I still have that yearning to love and guide them in the best way I can, no matter their age. From this common place, I want to help us all continue breaking free from the endless list of "shoulds" that modern motherhood demands. There's always a corner of our heart where fear, anger, comparison, insecurity, or control can become overwhelming. When you find yourself in those tough spots, don't lose hope. You already possess the key: the grace and love of Christ that equips you to keep dismantling your internal false images and replace them with liberating truths.

CHAPTER 15

Passing Along Patterns of Grace

Grace. Can it really be as simple as that? Jerry Bridges says, "Your worst days are never so bad that you are beyond the reach of God's grace. And your best days are never so good that you are beyond the need of God's grace."[19] This explanation encourages me not to let my good days or bad days as a mom dictate my willingness to keep accepting Christ's loving, complete work on my behalf—or more importantly, his willingness to keep offering it.

Though grace is simple, consistently living out the grace we receive from Christ requires a pattern of continual awareness and alignment with his truth. We are prone to forget, so we must humbly surrender again and again so we can once more rely completely upon his goodness alone to uphold us, care for us, and transform us. Brennan Manning wrote, "To live by grace means to acknowledge my whole life story, the light side and the dark. In admitting my shadow side I learn who I am and what God's grace means."[20] This shadow side echoes our inner false images, which are always being reconstructed within us. Thankfully, grace is always there to answer the lies with truth.

So how can we use this grace to dismantle the ideal image of ourselves that we've constructed in our minds?

First, write down your own detailed description of what your version of the ideal mom looks like. Does she never lose her temper? Does she keep the house spotless, even during chaotic times? Is she always in control of her kids' behavior? Does she look impeccable, stay fit, hold a successful job, and still whip up a homemade dinner every evening by five? Who is she really? Who are you trying to live up to? Be as specific as you can. Unless you consciously explore these inner perceptions in depth, it can be challenging to identify where you need to welcome God's grace to help you break free from these comparisons.

Once you begin to recognize how you truly view this imaginary figure and realize how influential she is in your thoughts, you can start shifting your focus away from comparing yourself to her. Establishing positive routines that bring you back to the awareness of being the Beloved Child in God's eyes becomes vital. This involves reminding yourself of the truths of who you are and who God is, truths that can become obscured by the shadows of self-doubt, exhaustion, or the weight of comparison.

For me, it's a source of strength to recall how God talks about himself and the different roles he has assumed to help and guide me. Each role teaches me how to rely on him in unique ways that counteract my false self-beliefs. Amazingly, when my untrue thoughts meet God's unwavering truths, it's like receiving a warm embrace from one of his most well-communicated roles in my life: the Good Shepherd. This makes me again feel secure, loved, and at peace.

This is where truth goes beyond mere religious phrases. It's genuine and powerful. When I confront my own brokenness and finally acknowledge just how much I need God, I begin actively receiving his love and support. If I avoid looking at my weaknesses, I can't fully see the beautiful changes he is bringing about. It's tough to face our flaws, but it's liberating to know they're redeemed by Christ's actions. So even if you don't feel like a supermom (which you shouldn't), remember that you've been given something even better: space to breathe and just be. God's grace creates this space within us, and it is something we can help pass along to our kids.

Feeling lost as a mom is normal. Remembering and returning to grace is like finding a comforting compass that guides us back to understanding who we are—and more importantly, *whose* we are. Grace reminds us of our true place in God's love and embrace.

Let me remind you again that the way our kids learn to navigate their own emotions and thoughts often mirrors how we navigate ours. We want to believe that our spoken lessons carry the most weight, but it's our way of being toward ourselves, God, and our kids that makes the most lasting impression. So then, whatever I desire my children to grasp and understand, I must authentically adopt and live out in my own life.

When we're in the act of parenting, we offer a glimpse of who we truly are inside. What's within us spills out in our thoughts, emotions, and actions. Along this journey, we'll undoubtedly make numerous mistakes, and no matter how hard we try, our kids will witness them. While we may aim to pass God's grace on to our children smoothly and gently, we must keep in mind that our own moments of falling short, along with our kids' slip-ups, will ultimately reveal what we're genuinely teaching them about grace. Remember, the one who doesn't mess up has no need for grace.

Your kids will not remember every story you read to them or every interaction or lecture you share with them throughout their lives, but they will vividly remember how you react when you stumble in front of them—and how you respond to their blunders as well. They'll remember if you showed up in unhealthy ways or if you were able to calmly connect with them on their level of pain or disorganization in the moment. Did you do so without shame and with an open embrace that proved you were both learning and growing together? And if you didn't at first, did you own your mistake and make it right?

Despite your kids' own choices and differences, they will likely follow your lead in terms of emotional regulation. This is why it is vital to consistently humble ourselves and let God reshape our inner world so that what's inside is actually healthy. Remember the story when I came down the stairs to find the kitchen a disaster? Nate and Libby immediately owned their mistake of not cleaning up as they said they would. But I also had to own my mistake of judging them based on the assumption that they were intentionally trying to hurt me. Like most conflicts, we all had something to own.

Next, we had to apologize. It is so important that moms learn to apologize when they mess up. Clinging to control by never admitting wrong may feel like you are keeping your authority intact, but it will only teach your children that once they're in charge of something or someone, they also never have to apologize. Moreover, they know that you sometimes make mistakes, so never apologizing teaches them that you're not willing to be honest with them. A heartfelt apology made with sincerity doesn't show weakness in a parent; in fact, vulnerability is a sign of strength and the only way to build meaningful connections. Because we're secure in knowing God forgives us and his goodness covers our mistakes, we can lead our family as the Chief Mistake Maker and Apologizer. By leading this way, they'll learn from us and do the same.

Apologizing might sound simple, but you can actually do more damage if you don't learn a few guidelines to the process. Make sure you address everyone involved, admit what you specifically did, acknowledge the hurt, and ask for forgiveness, which is more than just saying sorry.[21]

Reconciliation and repair occur when we admit the pain we've caused, face the outcomes, and change our ways. In the situation with the dishes, the kids didn't just apologize; they also showed it by cleaning up right away. After asking for forgiveness, they backed it up with actions. Real forgiveness lets our relationships move forward without lingering bad feelings. In this way, we can prevent small, lingering grudges from taking root and growing into something we don't want in our future relationships.

Every type can feel overwhelmed by conflicts like these in their own way. Knowing your type is essential because it allows you to see potential in even small conflicts. Conflicts are chances to be humble, show repentance, change your attitude toward your kids, and demonstrate how secure believers find rest in and take action out of grace.

Knowing this to be true, you can embrace the path that sometimes seems tougher—the path of growth—toward understanding your true self. The next part of the book will show you how the Enneagram can help as a guiding tool on this journey. Remember, you're uniquely crafted to reflect God's grace and truth in your life and story. Your life will enrich the lives of your kids and the generations that follow.

In the end, there is no unattainable standard to meet. No instant solutions to discover. No hidden formulas to unravel. You have the freedom to simply be who God has uniquely made you to be. Keep bringing your authentic self—your true colors—into your family life, all the while finding peace in God's unwavering love and abundant care for you and your loved ones.

You don't have to wait for perfection, Mom. Today—right now— you can bless the world with exactly who God has created you to be, letting your beautiful true colors shine. Then, you are free to allow these truths and this grace to flow into your relationship with your children, lovingly leading them into embracing and living out their own true colors, just as God intended.

Part 2

CHAPTER 16

Diving into the Nine Types of Parents

Now that we've explored so many aspects of our true colors through the lens of the Enneagram, can you see how parenting is a lot like creating a piece of art? Some days, your brushstrokes flow effortlessly, blending colors on the canvas as if guided by a divine hand. On other days, it feels like you're wrestling with your materials, trying to bring clarity to a smudged and chaotic scene.

That's where the second half of this book comes in—it's like your art supply shop for every parenting moment, complete with all the brushes, palette knives, and color tubes you could need. Each section is like adding another essential item to your artist's toolkit, helping to bring God's vision to life for you, your family, your friendships, and your community.

Don't worry. The tools we offer here aren't overwhelming or complicated—they are not an elaborate airbrush machine you've never used before. They're more like fine-tipped paintbrushes for adding delicate details or sponges to gently blend colors, subtly improving your masterpiece without radically changing it. These are the little tools that make your day-to-day life as a parent just a bit easier and much more enriching.

So keep this part of the book within arm's reach. Consider it a reliable artist's toolkit. I encourage you to refer back to it as often as you like. Over time, these tools will feel as natural in your hand as your favorite brush, providing consistent support through the intricate, rewarding art of parenting.

This part of the book is intended to be both practical and encouraging. You will not find quick fixes or formulas in these pages. Instead, you will find simple practices, and you'll increase your skill with them over time. Parenting is a journey full of wonder and joy but also setbacks. It's not a race, because a finish line doesn't exist. You will always be your child's parent. Instead, the goal is to shift your focus away from expectations and toward understanding what your child truly needs. To do this, you must look beyond outward behaviors to see the motivations beneath—and this begins with you. Becoming aware of your inner world and bringing healing and truth to your wounded stories is the first and most important step toward transforming the dynamics between you and your child.

Part 2 is not necessarily meant to be read cover to cover. Begin with your Enneagram type (if you don't know your type, this part of the book is for you!) and read through it to get the bigger picture of how your personality influences your parenting. Then, moving forward, you'll want to simplify things by reflecting on one small section at a time. Your core motivations are essential, and you can spend weeks becoming aware of when and how these motivations show up in your parenting. Then, circumstances in your life may draw you toward learning about your type's parenting blind spots or communication style. Remember, there is no formula. Even the prayer that closes each chapter can be said in stages. You can take a paragraph or a single sentence and meditate on it throughout the day or week. This book is written for you. What you do with it will reflect your personality and the time you have available.

As you read about your Enneagram type, you will find parenting examples written for young children and others written for older children. This book is for mothers and children of all ages. It's for grandmothers and great-grandmothers, too, because it's never too late to transform your family tree. The principles remain the same no matter what stage of parenting you find yourself in. So use these pages as a jumping-off point, and feel free to adjust the guide points to fit your unique child and circumstances.

Eventually, you'll want to read about all nine types because there are valuable insights for you in each one. Your Enneagram type is connected to many other Enneagram numbers, and you will see yourself in several of them (the reason for this is explained in the Enneagram Internal Profile chapter). Reading about the other Enneagram types will also help you understand other mothers. It can bring insight into your mom friendships so you can better encourage one another and benefit from one another's unique strengths.

If you know your own mother's type, reading about hers can provide context to your childhood story, and you can develop more compassion for her journey, even for the things that directly or indirectly caused you pain. If you're a grandmother, you can read about your child's type and see why she parents differently than you. Perhaps you worry that your daughter doesn't like your parenting style, but often, the reason she parents differently has more to do with her personality style and the lens through which she sees the world. Understanding one another's unique lens can lead to mutual support.

As we discussed in part 1, you can access our free Enneagram assessment, more information on core motivations and mistyping, and many other helpful resources at EnneagramForMoms.com. Now that you know how to find your main Enneagram type, it's time to dive into your inner world and bring clarity, compassion, and practical guidance to your parenting journey. As you embark on this road toward healing and transformation, your children will naturally absorb the positive changes that stem from your newfound self-awareness.

Let's begin nurturing the unique colors that make your family truly special!

CHAPTER 17

Type 1: The Principled Reformer

Conscientious | Orderly | Appropriate |
Ethical | Consistent | Judgmental

Parenting Core Motivations

Your **Core Fear** is that you (and your children) will be wrong, bad, evil, inappropriate, unredeemable, or corruptible.

Your **Core Desire** is that you (and your children) will have integrity, be good, ethical, balanced, accurate, virtuous, moral, and right.

Your **Core Weakness** is resentment—repressing anger that leads to continual frustration and dissatisfaction with yourself, your children, and the world for not being perfect.

Your **Core Longing** is to hear and believe that "you are good." You feel like you need to be perfect for yourself and your children, but striving for perfection is a never-ending pursuit you can't achieve alone. Know that your heart can rest because God forgives and loves you unconditionally as you are.

Primary Parenting Perspective

To achieve your core motivations, your primary focus is seeing errors, mistakes, and problems that need to be fixed. You are not seeking out these imperfections; they leap out at you and assault you. You believe parenting should be done rightly, accurately, and systematically, and you feel morally obligated to ensure your children become virtuous adults.

Parenting on Autopilot

The autopilot response of all parents is to guide their children to become little versions of their type's personality, because it's easier to parent a child to be just like you! Becoming aware of this tendency is a big step toward changing course and parenting with awareness so that you can respect your children's unique personalities and valid perspectives.

As a Type 1, you want to raise "Little Principled Reformers." You naturally desire your children to embody qualities such as self-discipline, fairness, reliability, and the ability to make wise choices. You work hard to instill a strong sense of responsibility in your kids, guiding them to become little adults who are conscientious and uphold high moral principles. You emphasize the importance of self-control, reasoning, and the ability to delay instant gratification. You envision your children as capable of striving for excellence, maintaining consistency, and making the right decisions.

While these are great qualities to teach your children, when parenting on autopilot, you may expect a maturity level that is inconsistent with their developmental abilities. Most of our children's actions and reactions come from unregulated emotions and are not deliberate moral choices. Furthermore, not all personalities are as naturally conscientious and self-disciplined as Type 1s. Knowing this can help you step back, parent with curiosity and grace, and allow your children to embrace their unique personalities as they develop wisdom and a moral compass with the help of your patient guidance.

Parenting Style

You are a highly intentional and responsible parent with firm boundaries. You have a clear inner knowledge of right and wrong, which allows you to be fair-minded, consistent, reasonable, and grounded. All of this gives your children a secure foundation to stand on, which is so important as they navigate a chaotic and confusing world. You are their anchor, and they know that tethered to you, they can safely explore the world without getting lost in it.

However, you may struggle to relax, play with, and enjoy your children due to your constant need to do what's right. Your children might feel pressure to be perfect, believing they must be "good" to be worthy of your love. The rope on your anchor can be too short, making it difficult for your children to find their own paths, values, and personalities.

The work of parenting is often unappreciated, which can trigger your core weakness of resentment. You struggle to admit you're angry because that would be "bad," and your core longing is to be good. Anger is a natural emotion, but it's important to process it in healthy ways. When you suppress or justify your anger, you can become perfectionistic and controlling of yourself and your children. Your children may experience your "helpful advice" as criticism or perceive you as demanding perfection from them, which can harm your relationship. The reality is that your heart truly longs to help, but your inner critic's focus on your children's behavior and not their hearts only increases the power struggle. Internally, you struggle to believe you are a good and worthy parent because your inner critic constantly finds fault with your parenting. To silence this berating voice, you strive never to make mistakes, which is impossible and exhausting.

When you learn to take your struggles and longings to God, you can begin to let go of the unrealistically high standards you hold for yourself and your children. You can parent with patient curiosity and grace, discovering what's under the behavior and connecting deeply with your children. Then your moral and purposeful nature can bring out the best in everyone, changing your family tree and making your home (and the world) a better place.

Levels of Alignment: Assessing Your Inner Well-Being

Aligned

Living in this healthy state, you forgo the chase for perfection to focus on a heartfelt connection. You lead with patience and moral integrity, and your curious and compassionate approach makes your children feel seen and loved for who they are. Free from the burden of condemnation, you readily offer forgiveness and grace, enriching your relationships and exemplifying divine love and patience to your family and beyond.

Misaligned

Living in this autopilot state, you listen to your inner critic's ceaseless critiques, creating an endless cycle of seeking perfection in yourself, others, and the world. This bondage to the unending pursuit of "getting it right" extends to your children. You interpret their behavior as moral failings, and they feel the weight of your expectations, which can cause them to feel nitpicked, judged, and unseen, growing up with the belief that they must appear perfect to receive love and acceptance. In trying to silence your inner critic by striving to do what is right, you inadvertently create an environment where perfection, not connection, becomes the currency for love.

Out of Alignment

Living in an unhealthy state, you fixate on the smallest imperfections in yourself and your children. You micromanage and assert control to gain relief from the tyranny of your inner critic. Your children feel smothered by criticism and judgment, feeling unknown or misunderstood, and, ultimately, unloved. In this parenting dynamic, your children can either lose their self-confidence, identity, and autonomy, or they can rebel and completely shut you out.

Childhood Message

As a child, you wanted to follow the rules, avoid getting in trouble, and be a good example. You were quiet, responsible, respectable, and you grew up quickly. Your relentless inner critic showed up early in life. Your parents rarely needed to discipline you because you were already internally punishing yourself for all your shortcomings. Your parents didn't know about your inner critic and thus didn't know how to correct or discipline you gently. As a result, you took what your parents said and internalized the criticism as a form of punishment, essentially punishing yourself twice.

Your childhood message is, "It's not okay to make mistakes." This was either directly said to you or is a message you perceived through interactions with others. It is hardwired in your mind, like a record player that constantly played when you were a child and continues to play into adulthood. It was painful then, and it is painful now. This message, however, is false. Of course it's okay and natural to make mistakes. Thankfully, God covers all your imperfections. When God looks at you, he sees his Beloved Child.

Parenting Struggles and Relationship Issues

- You can be rigid and inflexible, holding your children to strict standards they may not wholeheartedly share and forgetting that they are wired differently. (Growing up, children mirror their parents, but this doesn't mean they will have the same core motivations.)
- You may not allow enough "playtime" in your relationships, feeling that all spare time should be used for serious tasks like chores, education, and practicing skills.

- You can take on too much responsibility, increasing not only your own resentment but also the resentment of your child, who may feel controlled by your efforts or feel like they are second place to your to-do list.
- You may try to control your emotions and behaviors because you don't want to display emotions that are out of control or inappropriate. This can cause you to become uncommunicative, curt, depressed, and moody because of your repressed anger. You can forget that your child needs you to model how to accept, name, and regulate big emotions with kindness toward yourself. They don't have the ability to do it on their own.
- You strive for perfection because of your inner critic, and any negative feedback from others feels threatening. Your fear of criticism from others regarding your parenting decisions can bubble up and cause you to be nitpicky, scolding and correcting your children at every turn. You believe a false message that if your children appear good and perfect, you do as well. You (and your children) were never meant to carry this burden.

Communication Style

As parents, we can unknowingly look down on our children as lesser beings. Yes, we are older and wiser, and our children are not fully mature, but they are still human beings uniquely created by God. So when it comes to communication, be mindful of your focus on efficiency that can cause you to be too direct and disconnected from your emotions. Treat your children with respect, tenderness, and kindness, acknowledging their growth, level of maturity, and unique personality type. Aim to speak to your children when you are more self-aware, self-regulated, and able to attune to them and their needs. Of course, there will be bad days when you're far from that target and deep in your unhealthy communication style. Instead of falling into blame or shame, embrace grace and take the opportunity to apologize and repair.

When You're Not Doing Well

You can speak to your children in a teaching, correcting, and judgmental way, becoming easily irritated and opinionated while visibly showing your displeasure. Depending on their age, children may not always understand your words, but they can read and even feel your body language. When you find yourself in this unhealthy communication style, take a few deep breaths and let your body relax so your child sees that you have physically softened toward them. Remind yourself that you are God's Beloved Child, and so is your child. Going forward, you can begin to ask curious questions, becoming gentler and more flexible with your instructions and suggestions.

When You're Healthy

Your communication style assures your children that goodness will prevail for everyone, including them, which is a comforting gift. Your children can trust that you'll always be honest and sincere, treating them politely and respectfully. As you offer them connection and patient curiosity, they feel both supported and free to be their authentic selves. When your children make mistakes and stumble, as all people do, they know they can count on your graciously kind, well-thought-out insights and advice to help them find their way forward.

Steps Toward Parenting Growth

- Pause and ask clarifying questions instead of making judgmental statements about your child's behavior. Don't fall into the trap of negativity bias. Instead, always assume your child is trying their best. Become more curious about the *why* behind their behavior, not just the action.

– "Your teacher said you're behind on your homework. You're not in trouble. I just want to understand why. I know you're a smart kid, so whatever it is that's keeping you from doing your homework must feel pretty big right now."

• Adopt a standard of "good enough." This is difficult for Type 1s because you always see how things could improve, but progress isn't linear. Growing up is hard work, and parenting is a lifelong endeavor. Perfection is not the goal, connection is.

– For example, don't immediately point out what could be improved in your child's creative projects or athletic events. Instead, celebrate their progress and what they uniquely bring to the table. When they're ready to work on improvements, they'll come to you because you've proven you're a safe person to try and fail with. You make them feel good about their abilities.

• Recognize that two things can be true. Don't fall into power struggles by trying to shut down or change your child's "bad" emotions. When you were a child, black-and-white thinking and staying in control helped you navigate difficult circumstances. However, as an adult, you can hold and honor all perspectives and emotions—black, white, and all the shades of gray in between!

– For example, you can hold a boundary, and your child is allowed to feel and express frustration about it. One does not supersede the other. They can both exist in this moment.

• Take ownership of all your thoughts and feelings (don't repress or ignore emotions that feel "bad"). When your feelings get the best of you (which they will), and you say something harsh or critical, apologize. Tell your children they are not responsible for your unregulated reactions. Ask for feedback about how your critical words made them feel. Remember, connection neutralizes shame, and repair can happen fifteen minutes or fifteen years later. It's never too late!

– "I'm sorry about the way I spoke to you yesterday. I was feeling overwhelmed by all I had to do. I want you to know that it had nothing to do with you. I want to do better next time. Do you mind sharing how my words and frustration made you feel?"

- Achieve a healthier balance by allowing yourself guilt-free breaks to enjoy relaxation and play. It's perfectly fine to momentarily put aside your duties to recharge. Even just twenty minutes of prioritizing play can be vital for reviving your spirit and deepening the bond with your children. Let your child choose the activity, offering positive reinforcement. Stay fully engaged— set your phone aside, disregard household tasks, and don't dwell on upcoming responsibilities. Above all, unwind and enjoy the moment. Play is meant to be purely enjoyable, not a teaching opportunity.

- Share personal stories of times you made a mistake. In your child's eyes, you are a good and perfect person, which is a lot to live up to. Knowing that you made mistakes and had struggles growing up will help you connect on a deeper level, and it also helps neutralize their feelings of "not good enough."

– "Did I ever tell you about the time I . . ."

Your Blind Spot

When you're around those you are most comfortable with (mainly your family), you'll display misaligned characteristics you will not easily recognize. Your family notices, but you are usually blind to them, which is why we call them blind spots.* Being unaware of your blind spot characteristics can negatively affect your parenting and your connection with your children. To become aware of your blind spot, ask yourself the following questions:

- Do I ever demand that my children immediately meet my needs, criticisms, and desires?
  - Your inner critic can be so loud and demanding that you become equally demanding toward your children in your desperation to silence it. You can justify your needs as good and right. However, your demands are not for your children's benefit but rather to satisfy your overwhelmed emotions.
  - Ask yourself, "Are my requests really necessary? Does it need to be done immediately? Who benefits from this?"
- Do I find "escape hatches" (unhealthy indulgences) from my inner critic (and other responsibilities) to distract myself from the ongoing pressures I face?
  - Taking a break from your responsibilities and learning to rest and recharge are vital for a Type 1. However, when you turn to unhealthy or harmful habits to release stress, you're in your blind spot.
  - Instead of feeling guilty for this, remind yourself that desiring a break from your responsibilities is okay. Then direct that need toward healthier habits that help you rejuvenate.
- Have I ever experienced an irrational, immature urge to do something that isn't right, especially if I believe I can secretly get away with it?
  - When you find yourself in a "do as I say, not as I do"

---

* If you're familiar with the Enneagram, you already know that your blind spot displays the average to unhealthy attributes of your Type 7 Path. If you're wondering what Type 7 has to do with Type 1, you can find out more in chapter 28, "Your Enneagram Internal Profile (EIP)."

situation, or if you need to be secretive, you're in your blind spot. Again, remind yourself that these desires stem from a real need to experience freedom from your demanding inner critic and unending responsibilities.

– Children are great at pointing out our hypocrisy, so don't be surprised if they're the first to notice. This is, after all, your blind spot. Instead of rationalizing your behavior, use it as an opportunity to connect with your child and show that even parents make mistakes and need grace.

• Do I ever avoid feelings of pain, sadness, or disappointment, or find myself reframing a negative situation to sound more positive?

– As a Type 1, you can fall into toxic positivity when you fear that you or your child's feelings are bad or could lead to wrong thinking or decision-making. When you find yourself looking for the silver lining to solve your child's problems, or telling your child that feeling a certain way is inappropriate, pause and remind yourself that all emotions serve a purpose.

– God gave us emotions so we can process our experiences. He welcomes our wrestling and authenticity. Instead of avoiding your difficult feelings, use them as an opportunity to connect with your child by modeling how to process a full range of human experiences—the good and the bad.

AWARE (Mindfulness Exercise)

Awaken

Awaken to a thought or feeling. It could be:

• The belief that it's not okay to make mistakes.
• Feeling like you need to fix something.

- A critical thought from your inner critic about yourself or your child.
- A specific story from your childhood.
- A worry about your parenting, your relationship with your child, or your child's future.
- A feeling of resentment or a sense of guilt or shame. (Pay attention to your body. Do you feel tightness in your muscles or an inability to relax your posture? Are your eyes squinted and your jaw clenched?)

Welcome

Welcome and extend kindness to this part of you without guilt or shame. Remain curious, not critical. What starts as a thought is connected to a deeper feeling, and what begins as a feeling in your body has a story to share. Stay kind by remembering that this part of you has good intentions. It's trying to help you, even if it's causing you problems.

You can relax knowing that God is your advocate, and he embraces your weaknesses and mistakes with compassion and understanding. He accepts you as you are, and because of his grace, you can welcome and show kindness to all the parts of your heart.

Ask

Ask God to help you interpret what this part of you is trying to communicate and the motives behind these thoughts and feelings. How is this part of you connected to a wounding story from your childhood? Resist any urge to fix your situation. This is difficult for Type 1s because you like to perfect things. However, just as connecting is the goal for parenting, connecting is also the goal for AWARE. Give this part of your story space to be seen and heard.

Receive

Receive the forgiveness and compassion God offers you, allowing him to help you guide this misaligned and hurt part of your heart back to the truth. Spend a few minutes reading truths like these verses about God's compassion, freedom, and grace:

- "Come to me, all who labor and are heavy laden, and I will give you rest. Take my yoke upon you, and learn from me, for I am gentle and lowly in heart, and you will find rest for your souls. For my yoke is easy, and my burden is light." (Matthew 11:28–30 ESV)
- Therefore, there is now no condemnation for those who are in Christ Jesus. (Romans 8:1)
- For it is by grace you have been saved, through faith—and this is not from yourselves, it is the gift of God—not by works, so that no one can boast. (Ephesians 2:8–9)

Engage

Engage yourself, your children, and your parenting in a new way, with love, forgiveness, kindness, patience, and grace—the same way God engages with you. From this newly aligned place, your children will experience the same thoughtful curiosity and patience you are learning to show yourself.

Prayer for Type 1 Parents

Gracious and loving God, thank you for my unique role as a Type 1 mother. I am grateful for my sense of responsibility, desire to do what is right, and commitment to creating a virtuous and just environment for my children. I acknowledge that these qualities reflect your own heart. Thank you for the gifts of discernment and integrity I bring to my parenting role.

I recognize that my deep desire for perfection, order, and justice reflects you. At the same time, I acknowledge that my desires can become misaligned and harmful. Forgive me for the times I've responded critically to my children and demanded perfection to quiet my own inner critic. Thank you for satisfying my core longing for goodness by declaring me righteous, not because of my perfection but because of the perfection of the one who saved me.

Make me aware of my autopilot reactions that do not serve my children well so I can change how I engage with them. Help me bestow grace and tenderness toward my story so I can heal and change my family tree. As my Advocate and Mediator on this journey, you give me the freedom to try new things. I know I will never be perfect and that I can own and apologize when I make mistakes. Thank you that it's never too late to mend past wounds and reconnect with my children.

Today, I give you my hopes, fears, and aspirations for my children. Grant me the grace to embrace their uniqueness and foster an environment of love and understanding, allowing room for failure, growth, differences, and self-discovery. Help me recognize when I am parenting from my type in an unhealthy way, not seeing my children for who they are. And teach me to parent with open hands instead of clenched fists, trusting that you love my children even more than I do.

As I go about my day, help me reflect on my drive for excellence so I can learn to pause and be curious. Show me how to accept my thoughts and emotions, even when they feel bad. And help me model self-compassion and forgiveness so my children learn to embrace their own imperfections and cultivate resilience.

Please grow my community so I may find support, encouragement, and a sense of belonging in my parenting journey. Grant me the courage to talk about my anger with trusted people so I can learn to process it in honorable ways. Surround me with authentic, imperfect, and gracious mothers who sharpen me and encourage me to rest in your grace.

As I navigate the joys and challenges of parenting, help me embrace my story and the wounded parts of my heart and parent my children from a place of new awareness. Fill me with the wisdom and desire to repair. And keep my heart open to the beauty of imperfection and the gifts of play, rest, and connection. Amen.

CHAPTER 18

Type 2: The Nurturing Supporter

Thoughtful | Generous | Helpful | Demonstrative
| People-Pleasing | Possessive

Parenting Core Motivations

Your **Core Fear** is that others (and your children) will reject you, and you will be unwanted and thought worthless, needy, inconsequential, dispensable, or unworthy of love.

Your **Core Desire** is that you will be appreciated, loved, and wanted by others (and your children).

Your **Core Weakness** is pride—denying your own needs and emotions while using your strong intuition to discover and focus on the emotions and needs of others (and your children), confidently inserting your helpful support in hopes that they will say how grateful they are for your thoughtful care.

Your **Core Longing** is to hear and believe that "you are wanted and loved." You find yourself giving, serving, advising, and caring for others, including your children, to earn love and acceptance. However, you are already wanted and cherished just as you are, without having to do anything to receive this love. You're pursued by the unconditional love of God.

Primary Parenting Perspective

To achieve your core motivations, your primary focus is winning the approval of others and your children by feeling their emotions and fulfilling their needs. You project an image of being completely self-less, loving, and supportive to earn their love and affirmation. You are convinced that if you acknowledge and take care of your own needs, your children (or other parents) might view you as "selfish" and reject you.

Parenting on Autopilot

The autopilot response of all parents is to guide their children to become little versions of their type's personality, because it's easier to parent a child to be just like you! Becoming aware of this tendency is a big step toward changing course and parenting with awareness so that you can respect your children's unique personalities and valid perspectives.

As a Type 2, you want to raise "Little Nurturing Supporters." You want your children to embody kindness, compassion, thoughtfulness, and attentiveness to others. You nurture your kids to become little helpers, always eager to lend a hand and support those in need (including you). You model the importance of having a caring and giving nature and emphasize the importance of being there for others and positively affecting their lives. You envision your kids as compassionate individuals who will spread love and support, creating a nurturing environment for everyone they encounter.

While these are great qualities to teach your children, when parenting on autopilot, you can expect a thoughtfulness level that is inconsistent with their developmental abilities. Most of our children's actions and reactions come from unregulated emotions; they cannot be helpful or thoughtful in these moments. Furthermore, not all personalities possess the same superpower that Type 2s have in understanding and empathizing with others' feelings and needs. Knowing this can help you step back, parent with curiosity and grace, and allow your children to embrace their unique personalities as they develop compassion and determine their own approach to serving others.

Parenting Style

You prioritize relationships and ensure your children feel cared for and loved. You take a genuine interest in your children and come alongside them to serve, offer helpful advice, and nurture them. You're a natural motivator and encourager and are sensitive to your children's feelings. Your children feel safe opening up to you because of your warm, loving, empathetic presence. They know you will generously go the extra mile to support, help, and care for them.

However, you can struggle to believe that you are loved and wanted apart from the support you offer. In your attempt to fulfill a longing to be loved and appreciated, you can become people-pleasing and possessive in your parenting style, inserting your advice and perspective into your children's lives and violating their boundaries.

The work of parenting becomes a struggle when your children feel crowded by your efforts to help or don't want to help others as much as you do, which can trigger your core weakness of pride. You may believe you always know what's best, feeling hurt and insecure when your advice isn't accepted. In response, you can double down on your efforts to win your children over by people-pleasing, flattery, manipulation, and looking for more ways to make your children like you.

You believe it is your job to alleviate your children's disappointments and pain, which is a constant and impossible responsibility. You can also spend too much time outside your family, tending to the needs of friends and neighbors, and draining your energy and resources. This overwhelming burden to care is damaging when you don't adequately deal with your own needs. You convince yourself that you don't have any needs and ignore your feelings, resulting in burnout and resentment.

When you learn to take your struggles and longings to God and rest in his nurturing provision, you can begin to care for your needs without feeling guilt or shame. Having been restored by God's unconditional love and care, you can parent with curiosity and humility, honoring your children's unique personalities and connecting deeply with them through a non-anxious, nonintrusive presence. Then, your compassionate and caring nature can bring out the best in everyone, changing your family tree and making your home (and the world) a better place.

2

Levels of Alignment: Assessing Your Inner Well-Being

Aligned

Living in this healthy state, you selflessly love, care, and support both yourself and others without the constant need for external affection or approval. You're attuned to your own needs, open to asking for help, and mindful of maintaining appropriate boundaries by saying no when something is not your responsibility or could be harmful to you or your family. This loving stance stems from God's unconditional love for you and not from seeking others' validation.

Misaligned

Living in this autopilot state, you try to earn love and affirmation by confidently inserting your helpful support and advice. Your children can feel smothered by your efforts or second place to your service outside the home. You believe your motives come from a good place with no hidden agendas. However, you are creating dependencies so that others need you more. You hide your own needs but take offense when others don't notice that you need help, which confuses your family because they can't read your mind.

Out of Alignment

Living in this unhealthy state, you believe your worth depends solely on affirmations and appreciation, so you overstep your children's boundaries by insisting they receive your support and help even when it's not wanted or asked for. This can lead to martyr-like and passive-aggressive behaviors, causing you to overextend yourself emotionally and physically to the point of exhaustion or illness. Constantly discussing your ailments to gain attention without explicitly asking for what you need can result in your children either pushing you away—creating the very relational break you fear—or losing their autonomy in an effort to please you.

Childhood Message

As a child, you were caring, kind, warm, and focused on pleasing others. You expressed yourself in loving and generous ways so you could earn the love, attention, praise, and affection you were starving for. You intuitively knew other people's emotions and needs, allowing you to give the other person what they needed without their asking. Their shock, delight, and thankfulness for your service became addicting. You constantly read your parents' expressions and body language to assess their feelings toward you. When you couldn't sense you were loved or wanted, you'd consciously or unconsciously manipulate others into showing you affection by serving them. This began a pattern of taking care of others and neglecting your needs.

Your childhood message is, "It's not okay to have your own needs." This was either directly said to you or is a message you perceived through interactions with others. It is hardwired in your mind, like a record player that constantly played when you were a child and continues to play into adulthood. It was painful then, and it is painful now. This message, however, is false. God pursues and loves you unconditionally. You did nothing to earn his love. Resting in this truth allows you to acknowledge and tend to your emotions and needs. You can stop striving to gain appreciation by being the most loving, helpful, and supportive person because God says you are already lovable and accepted. You are his Beloved Child.

Parenting Struggles and Relationship Issues

- You may try too hard to please your children and receive their affection and appreciation. This unbalanced focus makes it difficult to create and hold the healthy boundaries you and your children need to thrive and grow.
- You can hover and not give your children adequate space. In response, they may push further away, creating the relational break you fear, or accommodate you, losing their sense of autonomy and limiting their ability to trust themselves and self-direct.
- You may expect your family to read your mind and know your needs and feel disappointed when they fail to anticipate them. But no one can accurately read a person's mind, and children are even less likely to read body language or interpret passive comments correctly. Clear communication is kind, especially to children still trying to figure out language and relationships.
- You can become possessive and jealous of your children, especially if you fear there is someone else they look up to or want to spend time with. This prevents your children from gleaning wisdom and love from "a village" of caretakers. While you should protect your children and not let them hang out with just anyone, you should also allow safe people to speak into your children's lives and help you carry the heavy load of parenting so you have space for self-care.
- You may think you are protecting and prioritizing your children by ignoring your hurt, needs, and anger. However, all emotions

come out one way or another. If they are not processed well, they will harm your relationship. Furthermore, your children need you to help them hold their big feelings so they can understand and process them. This will be difficult if you are uncomfortable with your own emotions and have not taken the time to understand and process your developmental story.

Communication Style

As parents, we can unknowingly look down on our children as lesser beings. Yes, we are older and wiser, and our children are not fully mature, but they are still human beings uniquely created by God. So when it comes to communication, be mindful of ways you might be talking down to them. Treat your children with respect, tenderness, and kindness, acknowledging their growth, level of maturity, and unique personality type. Aim to speak to your children when you are more self-aware, self-regulated, and able to attune to them and their needs. Of course, there will be bad days when you're far from that target and deep in your unhealthy communication style. Instead of falling into blame or shame, embrace grace and take the opportunity to apologize and repair.

When You're Not Doing Well

You can be passive-aggressive, manipulative, demanding, gossipy, and an oversharer. You insist that others listen to your helpful advice and act on it the way you believe is best and most loving. If others don't do what you have advised, you become hurt and martyr-like. Your children may not be the source of your hurt, but they may still naturally blame themselves for your mood, especially if you don't intentionally reassure them. When you find yourself in this unhealthy communication style, take a few deep breaths and let your body relax so your child sees that you have physically softened toward them. Remind yourself that you are God's Beloved Child, and so is your child. From this new place of awareness, you can apologize for your tone and explain to your child that your frustration and hurt is not about them. Going forward, you can maintain healthy boundaries by learning to say no so you don't overextend yourself.

When You're Healthy

Your communication style comforts and assures your children that your relationship is solid and that they remain your priority despite all the other needs you see in the world. You ask your children good questions and give helpful guidance without trying to control them or expecting their compliance. You're an empathetic listener and have a warm presence. Your children feel supported and free to be themselves because you affirm and encourage them. They can confidently explore the world and find their place in it because, in you, they have a secure place to return to. When your children make mistakes and stumble, as all people do, they know they can count on your help and compassionate care.

Steps Toward Parenting Growth

- Acknowledge that your overly confident advice-giving can contribute to tension, particularly when your child is dysregulated by their emotions and not ready for a solution. Often, children need their parents' presence and a hug more than their words.
  - "It looks like you have some big feelings. Can I sit with you?"
  - If the answer is yes, sit without giving advice. If their answer is no, don't take it personally. Give them space by saying:

"Okay. I'll check in on you later, or you can find me if you change your mind and want to talk about it."

- Pause before jumping in. When your children require assistance, ask curious questions that guide them toward solutions instead of inserting your help or taking over and doing it yourself.
  - "Wow. That's a tricky problem. You're working so hard to solve it, and I know you'll come up with a creative solution. What have you already tried? Why do you think it didn't work out? Have you considered this?"
- Learn to recognize your pride—the belief that you don't need anything. Humility for a Type 2 means you see your needs and voice them instead of waiting for people to read your mind. It also means accepting your painful feelings, including anger, sadness, and loneliness. Sharing your feelings and needs (in age-appropriate ways) with your children helps them see that it's okay to have big feelings, talk about them, and practice self-care.
  - "Mommy's having a grumpy day. It's not your fault. I'm tired and have a lot to do. But I need a break, so when you take a nap, I'll take one too."
  - For older kids, you can be more specific: "My boss said something to me that didn't feel good. I'm working through how I feel about it and how I should respond. I'm sorry I've been distracted and grumpy. I'll talk to my boss tomorrow so this doesn't continue to overwhelm me."
- Stay calm in heated discussions, and don't blame problems on others. Learn to recognize when your tone is too direct, demanding, or irritable. Repair with your child by taking responsibility for your words and actions and asking for forgiveness.
  - "I'm sorry about the way I spoke to you. I was feeling overwhelmed and wasn't taking care of myself. That has

nothing to do with you, and I want to do better next time. Do you mind sharing how my words made you feel?"

- Accept your deeper motives. Type 2s typically only see their motives as pure and fail to see the ways they are looking for love and appreciation. Recognize that two different things can be true at the same time. For example, you can be doing great and worthy deeds because you truly want to help people and also be doing them to receive love and appreciation. When you see your deeper motives, it's easier to say no so you're not spread too thin.
  - Ask yourself, "Deep down, what am I really wanting? What am I hoping to gain by saying yes to this person's needs?"
- Maintain healthy boundaries by recognizing that not every need is an emergency. Because of your compassion, you often quickly push your needs aside to tend to someone else. Our culture doesn't help, implying that mothers should become martyrs for their children, ignoring their self-care to prioritize their children's wants and desires. This results in burnout and resentfulness. You can't parent well on an empty tank.
  - Before you agree to help someone, picture an airplane. When you're on a plane with an emergency, you must put on your oxygen mask before helping others put on their masks.
  - Ask yourself two questions: (1) Do I have my mask on, or do I need some care first? (2) Do my children need help with their masks before I rush out to help others?

Your Blind Spot

When you're around those you are most comfortable with (mainly your family), you'll display misaligned characteristics you will not easily recognize. Your family notices, but you are usually blind to them, and that is why we call them blind spots.* Being unaware of your blind spot characteristics can negatively affect your parenting and connection with your children. To become aware of your blind spot, ask yourself the following questions:

- Do I ever feel deeply rejected because my children are not listening to or accepting my help?
  - When you're in your blind spot, you are extra sensitive to perceived slights, which you interpret as rejection. Because you're relational, it's hard when your kids want more independence, but this is a normal and healthy part of the parenting journey.
  - Ask yourself, "Is my child really rejecting me or simply asking for some space? Is this feeling of rejection connected to something deeper; that is, emotions or needs of my own that I have been avoiding?"
- Do I feel self-pity or like a martyr when my family doesn't understand how difficult it is to be constantly others-focused, helpful, and self-sacrificial?
  - Remember, to be truly understood, you must share your feelings and needs with others. Your family can't read your mind. Self-pity stems from an overwhelming amount of stress. Take a look at your schedule and who you've said yes to, and determine what you can take off your plate. Learning to say no and enforcing your boundaries will help you avoid self-pity.
- Do I withdraw as a form of manipulation when I feel moody, melancholy, or misunderstood to work out my emotions alone, protect my image of being the most helpful mother, or force my family to express their love and appreciation for me?

---

* If you're familiar with the Enneagram, you already know that your blind spot displays the average to unhealthy attributes of your Type Four Path. If you're wondering what Type Four has to do with Type Two, you can find out more in chapter 28, "Your Enneagram Internal Profile (EIP)."

– In your blind spot, difficult emotions that don't surface in public will pop up. When you withdraw, your children are left alone to wonder what is wrong and what they did to upset you (remember, children naturally blame themselves). It's important to take time for yourself, but before you withdraw, make sure your motives are for self-care and not to manipulate a response from your family.

– Let your children know you need some "me time" to rest and recharge, and you'll reconnect with them soon. Afterward, follow through on your promise to reconnect before starting other responsibilities.

• Do I daydream about becoming free of always needing to be helpful and selfless so that I can be my authentic self? Do I envy others who seem to have ideal lives and have more than me?

– Envy is a clear sign that you're in your blind spot. Social media increases this feeling because people and platforms only post their highlights, which are fabricated and filtered to appear perfect. It can seem like every other mom has the ideal life you're yearning for, but all moms struggle, and you're not seeing what happens behind their closed doors.

– Instead of focusing on what you don't have, practice gratitude for what you do have and fill yourself up with your favorite self-care practices.

AWARE (Mindfulness Exercise)

Awaken

Awaken to a thought or feeling. It could be:

• The belief that it's not okay to have your own needs.
• A desire to rush to help someone, flatter, or offer advice.

- A fear that you will be rejected or unlovable if you don't serve others.
- A specific story from your childhood.
- A worry about your parenting, your relationship with your child, or your child's future.
- A feeling of resentment, exhaustion, or shame. (Pay attention to your body. Do you feel tightness in your face? Are your eyebrows furrowed? Are you having a hard time relaxing even though you've been feeling ill?)

Welcome

Welcome and extend kindness to this part of you without guilt or shame. Remain curious, not critical. What starts as a thought is connected to a deeper feeling, and what begins as a feeling in your body has a story to share. Stay kind by remembering that this part of you has good intentions. It's trying to help you, even if it's causing you problems.

You can relax knowing that you are wanted and loved unconditionally and perfectly by God, so you can loosen your grip on needing to be constantly valued by others. He loves you as you are, and because of his grace, you can welcome and show kindness to all the parts of your heart.

Ask

Ask God to help you interpret what this part of you is trying to communicate and the motives behind the thoughts and feelings. How is this part of you connected to a wounding story from your childhood? Resist any urge to fix your situation. This is difficult for Type 2s because you are used to running to the rescue to fix things for other people. However, just as connecting is the goal for parenting, connecting is also the goal for AWARE. Give this part of your story space to be seen and heard without trying to help it.

Receive

Receive the forgiveness and compassion God offers you, allowing him to help you guide this misaligned and hurt part of your heart back to the truth. Spend a few minutes reading truths like these verses about God's unconditional love and care:

- The LORD your God is in your midst, a mighty one who will save; he will rejoice over you with gladness; he will quiet you by his love; he will exult over you with loud singing. (Zephaniah 3:17 ESV)
- "Come to me, all you who are weary and burdened, and I will give you rest. Take my yoke upon you and learn from me, for I am gentle and humble in heart, and you will find rest for your souls. For my yoke is easy and my burden is light." (Matthew 11:28–30)
- "I have loved you with an everlasting love; I have drawn you with unfailing kindness." (Jeremiah 31:3)

Engage

Engage yourself, your children, and your parenting in a new way with humility, forgiveness, healthy boundaries, patience, and grace—the same way God engages with you. From this newly aligned place, your children will experience the same unconditional love and care you are learning to show yourself.

Prayer for Type 2 Parents

Gracious and loving God, thank you for my unique role as a Type 2 mother. I am grateful for my nurturing spirit, ability to empathize, and selflessness in caring for my children. I acknowledge that these qualities reflect your own heart. Thank you for allowing me to demonstrate your love to my family.

I recognize that my selfless nature and deep desire to care for others reflect you. At the same time, I acknowledge that my helpfulness can become misaligned and harmful. Forgive me for the times I've not respected my child's unique personality by hovering too closely, manipulating them to receive affection, or demanding too much. Thank you for satisfying my core longing to be wanted and loved, not because of my helpfulness but because of your unconditional love for me.

You know I am sensitive to the feelings and needs of others, often putting their well-being before my own. Help me to be aware of my own needs and limitations. Remind me that caring for myself is not a detriment to caring for others but gives me the energy and creativity to help others with my overflow. Give me the wisdom to practice self-compassion and seek support when needed.

Make me aware of my autopilot reactions that do not serve my children well so I can change how I engage with them. Grant me discernment in setting healthy boundaries, the courage to say no when necessary, and the ability to prioritize my well-being without guilt. Teach me to find joy in creating space for myself just as much as I enjoy serving others, so I can model balance for my children. I know I can better care for my family when I care for myself.

I pray for my relationship with my children. I feel sad and scared when I see my kids growing up and needing me less, and I wonder if I'm losing my place in their lives. Help me encourage their individual journey and give them the space they need. Remind me that their independence is a sign that I've nurtured them well and equipped them with the skills and confidence they need to handle life. Help me trust that our connection will remain strong despite our roles shifting.

Please grow my community so I may find support, encouragement, and a sense of belonging in my parenting journey. Grant me the courage to talk about my feelings and needs while also being mindful and respectful of others who are not in the room. As I lean on your wisdom, reveal what is mine to share and what is best left unsaid. Put trusted people in my life so I can learn to process my emotions, accept help, and care for myself. Surround me with authentic, imperfect, and gracious mothers who respect my boundaries and care for me as much as I care for them.

As I vulnerably embrace my story and the wounded parts of my heart, help me parent my children from a place of new awareness. Fill me with the humility and desire to repair, and keep my heart open to the immeasurable impact of loving without strings attached since I know that all the love and acceptance I need comes fully from you. As I navigate the joys and challenges of parenting, grant me the gifts of self-care, rest, and deep connection. Amen.

2

CHAPTER 19

Type 3: The Admirable Achiever

Efficient | Accomplished | Motivating |
Advocate | Driven | Image-Conscious

Parenting Core Motivations

Your **Core Fear** is being exposed as or thought incompetent, inefficient, or worthless as a mother or failing to be or appear successful at parenting.

Your **Core Desire** is having a high status and respect and being an admired, successful, and valuable mother.

Your **Core Weakness** is deceit—deceiving yourself into believing you are only the image of motherhood you present to others and embellishing the truth by putting on a polished persona for everyone (including yourself and your children) to see and admire.

Your **Core Longing** is to hear and believe that "you are loved and valued for simply being you." You feel pressured to be the best parent and look like a successful mother. However, God has already accomplished all you need. You are now liberated to rest and simply "be" with your children.

Primary Parenting Perspective

In order to achieve your core motivations, your primary focus is accomplishing tasks and goals so you can gain recognition, approval, and admiration from your family and other parents. In every situation, you focus on what needs to happen or how you (or your children) need to adapt to appear successful and prestigious.

Parenting on Autopilot

The autopilot response of all parents is to guide their children to become little versions of their type's personality, because it's easier to parent a child to be just like you! Becoming aware of this tendency is a big step toward changing course and parenting with awareness so that you can respect your children's unique personalities and valid perspectives.

As a Type 3, you want to raise "Little Admirable Achievers." You expect your children to excel in various tasks, fulfill family ambitions, achieve their goals, and be physically attractive and popular. You inspire your kids to become little stars, radiating brilliance in every area of their lives, whether academics, extracurricular interests, or social interactions. You encourage your children to strive for success, setting their sights on becoming role models and achieving recognition for their accomplishments. You envision your kids meeting very high standards.

While these are great qualities to teach your children, when parenting on autopilot, you may focus too heavily on "doing" and neglect rest. Feeling tired and pressured to succeed can dysregulate their emotions and cause tension and misunderstanding in your relationship, especially if your child has a more withdrawn personality and is less competitive. Knowing this can help you step back, parent with curiosity and grace, and allow your children to embrace their unique personalities as they develop their interests and skills and decide what they want to do with them.

Parenting Style

You encourage your children and help them build confidence in their abilities. You're good at making goals and solving problems, and your children know they can count on your help when they can't see a way forward. Your many connections and optimistic nature set your family up for success. You teach your children how to adapt quickly to any situation or scenario, confidently work toward their goals, and solve any problem that pops up along the way. You are their greatest cheerleader.

However, in our fast-paced and comparison-driven society, there are limitless opportunities for you (and your children) to achieve more, drive results, and excel in new ways. You struggle to keep up with the belief that you must be a successful mother in every aspect of parenting. Burdened to impress the people around you, you live under constant pressure to measure your worth by external achievement. You can also become a workaholic in your career, causing you to miss out on spending time with your children and making them feel second best to your career goals.

The work of parenting might leave you feeling worthless or incapable and can trigger your core weakness of deceit. You hide the less-becoming parts of yourself that you don't want your children or other people to see, which prevents you from building genuine relationships. You want to portray only a successful image, and in doing so, you become unaware of who you authentically are at the core of your being and struggle to share your true self with your family.

You are excessively driven and image-conscious, which causes you to be competitive and self-promoting and constantly compare yourself to other mothers and your children to other kids. This eventually leads to burnout because if you are only as good as your last accomplishment (or your child's last win), you're stuck on a treadmill that never stops. This exhausting pace is detrimental to your relationships.

When you learn to take your struggles and longings to God, you can begin to see that you are loved and valued for who you are, not what you accomplish and produce. This helps you slow down and be fully present. You can parent with confidence, enthusiasm, and determination, no longer putting pressure on your children but inspiring them. Then your adaptable and driven nature can bring out the best in everyone, changing your family tree and making your home (and the world) a better place.

Levels of Alignment: Assessing Your Inner Well-Being

Aligned

Living in this healthy state, you balance your work and family life and take off your achieving masks to reveal your authentic self. You can feel, name, and express your emotions openly with your family. You become a humble team player and champion of your children and other parents. You use your incredible talents and skills to solve problems efficiently and productively, benefiting others as much as yourself. You help your children become the best versions of themselves, finding joy in authentic excellence without needing external praise or admiration.

Misaligned

Living in this autopilot state, you believe you must earn love and admiration by excelling in all aspects of life, including parenting. You shape-shift to project a successful and admirable image, masking your true emotions from yourself and others, and you encourage your children to do the same. This focus on success and accomplishment puts your children under immense pressure to excel, maintain a popular image, and attain social elite status for praise and recognition. Consequently, this strains relationships and prevents authentic connections with your children and others.

Out of Alignment

Living in this unhealthy state, you constantly boast, fabricate, and embellish stories about yourself, your achievements, and your family to gain admiration from others. Believing your worth hinges on people's opinions, you look out for yourself and become extremely competitive. You refuse to admit when you are wrong or reveal anything that might diminish your image, which makes it hard for you to repair with your children or model honesty. Presenting a favorable image all the time is exhausting. It's also exhausting for your children because you insist they look and perform at the highest level so you can be admired through their accomplishments. If they fail, you may shame or belittle them.

Childhood Message

As a child, you sensed or were told that you needed to set aside your identity and become the kind of person that important people in your life deemed successful and admirable. This caused you to fixate on achieving, performing, and showing off your accomplishments. You conformed to what your family or culture said was the preferred image, even if this meant that you had to discount your true self. You believed this was necessary to gain the recognition you longed for. Ultimately, you feared that your parents, friends, coaches, and other important figures would overlook or forget you if you did not excel in every area of life. This means you had to be the best athlete, straight-A student, and likable kid.

Your childhood message is, "It's not okay to have your own feelings and identity." This was directly said to you or is a message you perceived through interactions with others. It is hardwired in your mind, like a record player that constantly played when you were a child and continues to play into adulthood. It was painful then, and it is painful now. This message, however, is false. Because you are God's Beloved Child, you no longer need to strive to become anyone else. You don't have to chase after success to receive God's love. You already have it. And you have the perfect status you desire because he accomplished it and gave it to you. This frees you from the tyranny of believing you always have to be the best. You can now rest and connect with your true self and your family.

Parenting Struggles and Relationship Issues

- You tend to present a favorable image instead of your authentic and genuine self. The people in your life may sometimes say, "Wait a second. That's not necessarily true. Is this the real you? Who are you?" Children are less attuned to your subtle shape-shifting, but as they mature, they will notice inconsistencies in who they know you to be and who you present to the world. This can cause relational disconnection because they wonder if they really know you.
- You can become a workaholic because you fear that people only want you for your looks or abilities, so you put all your effort into being the best. You can easily make excuses for this behavior, especially in a society that values accomplishments. However, when you're constantly working for the next "win," you miss out on simply being with your children and having fun without checking off a goal.
- You want your family to be proud of you and your accomplishments. However, like everyone, you have parts of yourself that are less outstanding or acceptable. Fearing potential rejection, you may prevent others (including your children) from getting too close to you by keeping yourself and your family busy and distracted by goals.
- To avoid rejection, you may shape-shift to embody the admirable qualities of other mothers you desire to be instead of

being your authentic self. Our social media and platform-driven society makes this even more difficult because you constantly see picture-perfect families you feel you need to live up to, which is an exhausting and unattainable goal.

- You want to be loved for simply being you without needing to accomplish anything. However, approval and admiration become a safer substitute for authenticity and vulnerability. Taking off your achievement masks not only allows your children to see the real you but also allows you to clearly see them for who they truly are and not only who you hope they will become.

Communication Style

As parents, we can unknowingly look down on our children as lesser beings. Yes, we are older and wiser, and our children are not fully mature, but they are still human beings uniquely created by God. So when it comes to communication, be mindful of your focus on efficiency that causes you to be too direct and disconnected from your emotions. Treat your children with respect, tenderness, and kindness, acknowledging their growth, level of maturity, and unique personality type. Aim to speak to your children when you are more self-aware, self-regulated, and able to attune to them and their needs. Of course, there will be bad days when you're far from that target and deep in your unhealthy communication style. Instead of falling into blame or shame, embrace grace and take the opportunity to apologize and repair.

When You're Not Doing Well

Your tone can be short and impatient, especially if you're interrupted by your children. You speak sharply from a desire to solve their issues quickly and efficiently so you can get back to focusing on your goals. The opposite happens when you fear you're not measuring up or someone points out your failures. Your conversations become self-promoting and lengthy, and you blame circumstances or other people (including your children) for getting in the way. When you find yourself in one of these unhealthy communication patterns, take a few deep breaths and let your body relax so your child sees that you have physically softened toward them. Remind yourself that you are God's Beloved Child, and so is your child. From this new place of awareness, you can apologize for your tone and explain to your child that your frustration is not about them. Going forward, you can be more mindful of work-life balance, enabling you to be more patient and available to your children.

When You're Healthy

Your communication style is clear, straightforward, confident, optimistic, and encouraging. You help your children find solutions and discover the value of teamwork. Your children feel supported, seen, and self-confident because you are their greatest cheerleader. When your children make mistakes and stumble, as all people do, they know they can count on your abilities, resilience, and connections to help them overcome any challenge.

Steps Toward Parenting Growth

- Recognize that your children may not be as driven, quick, and efficient as you are. You can get irritated with the slowness of others because you're fast at everything, but not everyone is created this way. Demonstrate understanding, patience, and acceptance of your child through gentle, motivating words.
  – "I'm sorry that I'm rushing you. I know I have a lot more

energy and can sometimes push you to finish things too quickly. I get excited because I know you're capable of doing this, but I also realize I need to have patience so this is fun for both of us. Let's take a ten-minute break before we continue."

- Allow your children to give you feedback about your parenting without making excuses or blaming them when you feel like you've failed.

  – All parents make mistakes, but you have more difficulty accepting failure due to your strong drive for success and achievement. Learning to embrace failure doesn't mean settling for mediocrity or giving up on your goals. It means embracing the inevitable setbacks and using them as opportunities for growth, resilience, and, ultimately, becoming a more authentic and compassionate person.

- Ask about your children's lives and then listen well. You can get so focused on tasks and goals that you lose sight of relationships. It's important to connect and draw out what your children think and feel and to be available when they are ready to talk.

  – When your child is speaking, put aside distractions (such as electronic devices) and offer your undivided attention. Active listening involves not only hearing the words your child is saying but also understanding their emotions and underlying messages. Pay close attention to their tone, body language, and nonverbal cues, and show empathy by refraining from rushing them to fix the situation or taking over to do it yourself.

  – Repeat back to them to show you're actively listening: "I hear you saying you've been overwhelmed with school and soccer practice. It sounds like you have a lot on your plate right now, and it feels like you're constantly trying to keep up."

- Create a healthy work-life balance by physically and mentally disconnecting from your work. When you're resting from your work, your children have an opportunity to get to know the real you.
  - "I'm sorry for being distracted and not fully present when I'm at home with you. You are important to me, and I want to change that. How does my distraction make you feel? You can be honest with me. Let's also write down some ideas on what we can do together."
  - Accomplish goals for the benefit of others. You are incredible at seeing the potential in others (including your children and other moms) and motivating them to be the person God has called them to be. Focus on bringing them into the spotlight since you no longer need to monopolize the spotlight to feel worthy or loved.
  - Actively listen to your child's (or another mom's) ideas, goals, and interests, and support them in pursuing them. Be there to cheer them on, guide them when needed (without pushing them too hard), and provide them with love and support no matter their success or talent level.
- Connect with at least one other mom with whom you can be completely honest and share your successes, failures, sadness, loneliness, and joys. This helps you reveal your authentic self and see that you are loved, even when not presenting the most favorable image.
  - In moments of disappointment or frustration, you experience a mix of emotions, including sadness, anger, or self-doubt. It's important to acknowledge and process these emotions rather than trying to mask them or push them aside. It can help to process them with another mom who is gracious, nonjudgmental, and understands the social pressures and unrealistic expectations you face.

3

Your Blind Spot

When you're around those you are most comfortable with (mainly your family), you'll display misaligned characteristics you will not easily recognize. Your family notices, but you are usually blind to them, and that is why we call them blind spots.* Being unaware of your blind spot characteristics can negatively affect your parenting and your connection with your children. To become aware of your blind spot, ask yourself the following questions:

- Do I express my frustration, dissatisfaction, and dread when my anxiety rises?
  - You're typically optimistic and confident, especially outside of the home. However, when struggling with anxiety, you'll complain and display a negative attitude around your family that you don't typically reveal to others. Your family can pick up on this energy and become on edge or uneasy, affecting the overall atmosphere. This can make it challenging for your children to relax and feel at ease around you.
  - You shouldn't wear a positive mask all the time. Your children should see you model how to process difficult emotions. But in your blind spot, you can unfairly overwhelm your family with your anxieties. A trusted friend, coach, or counselor can help you process your fears and frustrations so you don't dump them all at home.
- Do I struggle with self-doubt and confusion, leading me to seek guidance and support from others?

---

* If you're familiar with the Enneagram, you already know that your blind spot displays the average to unhealthy attributes of your Type 6 Path. If you're wondering what Type 6 has to do with Type 3, you can find out more in chapter 28, "Your Enneagram Internal Profile (EIP)."

- You're typically in forward motion, confident in reaching your goals. However, when you're in your blind spot, you experience self-doubt and turn to perceived experts to help you find your way. This can pressure your family to live up to whatever advice or ideals you've turned to for help, and they may start to believe that success is unattainable or that their efforts will always fall short.
- Ask yourself, "Is this advice encouraging realistic expectations for myself and my family? Where can I find joy and contentment in this moment rather than solely focusing on improvement?"

- Do I strongly react when blamed or accused of something?
  - Any challenge to your desired self-image can trigger feelings of failure, guilt, and self-doubt, which is difficult for you to accept. But when you default to defending yourself, your children will also learn not to take responsibility for their mistakes.
  - When you feel a need to protect your self-image, remember that your children are watching. Ask yourself, "Is this defense true, or am I using blame to distract, defend, and protect my self-image? How can I best model honesty and accountability to my children?"

- Do I avoid trying things I think I (or my child) might fail at?
  - If you sense your child is not naturally talented at something, you may discourage them from pursuing it because watching your child fail is uncomfortable for you. You also struggle with impatience and don't enjoy the time it takes to develop new skills. In your blind spot, you prefer activities you know your child will excel at quickly.
  - Not allowing your child to take calculated risks and try new things can stunt your child's personal growth and self-discovery. Even if the outcome is not a huge success,

the experience can offer your child valuable insights. By working together to gain new skills, you can overcome fears of failure and connect on a deeper, more vulnerable level.

AWARE (Mindfulness Exercise)

Awaken

Awaken to a thought or feeling. It could be:

- The belief that it's not okay to have your own feelings and identity.
- Feeling like you need to achieve a goal and you're only as good as your last accomplishment.
- Fear of failure, shame, or being exposed.
- A specific story from your childhood.
- A worry about your parenting, your relationship with your child, or your child's future, or comparing yourself or your child to others you think are more successful.
- A feeling of irritation, dissatisfaction, or shame. (Pay attention to your body. Do you look put together even though you feel tired and overworked? Are your shoulders set high and unrelaxed? Are you ignoring a heavy feeling in your gut?)

Welcome

Welcome and extend kindness to this part of you without guilt or shame. Remain curious, not critical. What starts as a thought is connected to a deeper feeling, and what begins as a feeling in your body has a story to share. Stay kind by remembering that this part of you has good intentions. It's trying to help you, even if it's causing you problems.

These emotions may feel uncomfortable and unproductive, but the opposite is true. Becoming comfortable with your feelings allows you to connect deeper with yourself and your children. Because of God's great love for you, you can relax, unmask, and stop chasing after success. You can let go of the need to constantly strive as a "human doing" and instead focus on simply living today as a "human being." Resting in God's grace, you can welcome and show kindness to all the parts of your heart.

Ask

Ask God to help you interpret what this part of you is trying to communicate and the motives behind the thoughts and feelings. How is this part of you connected to a wounding story from your childhood? Resist any urge to fix your situation or jump out of the exercise, perhaps distracting yourself with a goal. This can be difficult for Type 3s because you always want to be achieving. However, just as connecting is the goal for parenting, connecting is also the goal for AWARE. Give this part of your story space to be seen and heard.

Receive

Receive the forgiveness and compassion God offers you, allowing him to help you guide this misaligned and hurt part of your heart back to the truth. Spend a few minutes reading truths like these verses about God's love for you and how much he values you for simply being you:

- "Look at the birds of the air; they do not sow or reap or store away in barns, and yet your heavenly Father feeds them. Are you not much more valuable than they?" (Matthew 6:26)
- "Come to me, all who labor and are heavy laden, and I will give you rest. Take my yoke upon you, and learn from me, for I am gentle and lowly in heart, and you will find rest for your

souls. For my yoke is easy, and my burden is light." (Matthew 11:28–30 ESV)

- But you are a chosen people, a royal priesthood, a holy nation, God's special possession, that you may declare the praises of him who called you out of darkness into his wonderful light. (1 Peter 2:9)

Engage

Engage yourself, your children, and your parenting in a new way, with patience, humility, and authenticity—the same way God engages with you. From this newly aligned place, your children will experience the same unconditional love and acceptance you are learning to show yourself.

Prayer for Type 3 Parents

Gracious and loving God, thank you for my unique role as a Type 3 mother. I am grateful for my optimistic spirit, capacity to adapt to any situation, and ability to achieve for the good of my family. I acknowledge that these qualities reflect your own heart. Thank you for allowing me to demonstrate your hope and triumph.

I recognize the pressure I put on myself to succeed and the image I strive to maintain. Grant me discernment to know when to push forward and when to pause—when to strive and when to rest. Align my ambitions with your will. Teach me to set healthy boundaries that prioritize the well-being of myself and my children. Help me trust in your divine plan for my family.

In moments of self-doubt and fear of failure, remind me of your unwavering love and acceptance. Help me embrace my vulnerabilities and shortcomings, knowing my achievements do not define my worth. Guide me to be authentic in my parenting, showing my children the beauty of imperfection and the importance of genuine connection.

Show me that true success comes from using my gifts and talents to serve others, not from seeking recognition or accolades. Help me model humility, grace, and compassion to my children so that they may learn and model it for themselves.

Make me aware of my autopilot reactions that do not serve my children well so I can change how I engage with them. In the midst of busyness and distractions, remind me to be fully present for my children. Grant me the ability to truly listen, offer comfort and support, and create a safe space for them to express their thoughts and emotions. Help me celebrate their unique qualities and nurture their individuality without pushing them to be the best.

Please grow my community so I may find support, vulnerability, and a sense of belonging in my parenting journey. Grant me the courage to take off my achieving masks so I can reveal my true self and share my genuine emotions. Surround me with authentic, imperfect, and gracious mothers who accept the real me and encourage me to rest and be present with them.

As I vulnerably embrace my story and the wounded parts of my heart, help me parent my children from a place of new awareness. Fill me with patience and humility and the desire to repair, and keep my heart open to the immeasurable impact of loving my children for who they are, not for their accomplishments. As I navigate the joys and challenges of parenting, grant me the gifts of balance, rest, and authentic connection. Amen.

CHAPTER 20

Type 4: The Introspective Individualist

Authentic | Creative | Expressive | Deep
| Sensitive | Temperamental

Parenting Core Motivations

Your **Core Fear** is that you (and your children) will be inadequate, plain, mundane, defective, insignificant, flawed, or emotionally cut off from your authentic self.

Your **Core Desire** is to be a unique, special, and authentic mother (and raise unique, special, and authentic children).

Your **Core Weakness** is envy—feeling that you're tragically flawed, something foundational is missing inside you, and that other mothers possess qualities you lack.

Your **Core Longing** is to hear and believe that "you are seen and loved for exactly who you are—special and unique." You feel like you're missing something vital and don't fit in with others. However, God loves and sees you for who you truly are, so you are freed from trying to prove you are unique.

Primary Parenting Perspective

To achieve your core motivations, your primary focus is seeing what is missing in your life (and in your family) so you can continue longing for it. It's as if you have already experienced what real beauty, authenticity, and depth bring to life, and you long to experience it again because it was so deeply satisfying.

Parenting on Autopilot

The autopilot response of all parents is to guide their children to become little versions of their type's personality, because it's easier to parent a child to be just like you! Becoming aware of this tendency is a big step toward changing course and parenting with awareness so that you can respect your children's unique personalities and valid perspectives.

As a Type 4, you want to raise "Little Introspective Individualists" who embrace their sensitive nature, explore their artistic abilities, delve into their emotions, and develop a profound understanding of themselves and others. You foster genuine empathy in your children to be kind-hearted listeners who can truly connect with the emotions and needs of others. You inspire your children to delve into the depths of their inner world and express themselves authentically. You envision them using their individuality to bring vulnerability and beauty to the world.

While these are great qualities to teach your children, when parenting on autopilot, you may expect a depth of emotional understanding that is inconsistent with their developmental abilities. Most of our children's feelings and reactions come from unregulated emotions they do not fully understand, and they need you to hold their big emotions for them. Furthermore, not all personalities are naturally empathetic and self-reflective, or value creativity as much as Type 4s. Knowing this can help you step back, parent with curiosity and grace, and allow your children to embrace their unique personalities as they get to know themselves and their special way of connecting with the world.

Parenting Style

You are an authentic, creative, and expressive parent, living primarily in your imagination and feelings. You introduce your children to a unique, beautiful, and deep world. You're comfortable embracing a wide range of emotions and experiences, helping your children navigate their inner worlds. You're in tune with the profound despair and suffering around you, bravely pressing into those depths to discover rich meaning, and you help your children do the same.

However, you have a hidden, romanticized self and vision of the mother you passionately desire to become. This idealized self is marked by immense creativity, social adeptness, and unique significance. You measure yourself against this idealized version and constantly feel like you come up short. Feeling flawed makes you doubt if others, including your children, can truly understand and love you. To fill this void, you strive to embody the version of yourself you've created in your head, but you can get lost in your daydreams and miss opportunities to connect with your children.

The work of parenting might feel mundane and less than ideal for you, triggering your core weakness of envy. You may believe other families and mothers have it better, and you can experience shame when comparing yourself to them. Feeling defective makes you long for the qualities others possess. This fosters an "us vs. them" mentality, hindering you and your children from connecting with others and benefiting from the support of a nurturing community.

You can become self-absorbed and temperamental in your attempt to find your unique significance. You are painfully self-conscious, spending a great deal of energy ruminating on how different you are from other mothers. You navigate feelings of self-hatred, emptiness, and despair. Even though you may not be voicing any of these feelings, your resulting moods can contribute to the overall atmosphere of your home, making it more tense, unpredictable, or prone to conflicts, which can affect your children's sense of stability and security.

When you learn to take your struggles and longings to God, you can begin to let go of becoming an idealized mother with idealized children. You can parent with curiosity and emotional balance, discovering all the great attributes you and your children already possess. Then your deep and empathetic nature can bring out the best in everyone, changing your family tree and making your home (and the world) a better place.

Levels of Alignment: Assessing Your Inner Well-Being

Aligned

Living in this healthy state, you enjoy your innate creativity, inspire others, and experience your vast and beautiful emotions with a balanced perspective. You create space for your children to share their deepest emotions and needs, encouraging them to explore their authentic selves. You know you lack nothing, and what you sometimes feel is missing is actually already yours. Therefore, you can confidently embrace your role as an incredible mom, sharing your abundant gifts with your children and those around you.

Misaligned

Living in this autopilot state, you exaggerate your uniqueness to get attention and affection. You believe you are missing something foundational that other mothers have, which causes envy. Always searching for your unique self in your internal world of emotions and imagination causes you to withdraw from your children. You feel lonely, inadequate, and misunderstood, and you can unintentionally make your children feel the same way in your absence.

Out of Alignment

Living in this unhealthy state, you feel unlovable and not valued for your authentic self. You strive harder to be unique and set apart so others will see and value you. This causes you to be temperamental and moody with your children. You plunge into sadness, despair, and self-absorption, believing no one will ever understand you. Feeling misunderstood, you withdraw further, impairing your children's attachment to you.

Childhood Message

As a child, you often felt different from your parents, siblings, and those around you. You did not see yourself reflected in your parents, and this caused you to feel disconnected and misunderstood. You didn't feel that your parents took an interest in knowing you completely or even tried to understand how you were unique and special. This caused you to feel rejected, abandoned, and lonely, as if there was something fundamentally missing and flawed about you. Since you couldn't see yourself in your parents, you turned inward to find your authentic self. You still desire to show the world how unique and special you are.

Your childhood message is, "It is not okay to be too much or not enough." This was directly said to you or is a message you perceived through interactions with others. It is hardwired in your mind, like a record player that constantly played when you were a child and continues to play into adulthood. It was painful then, and it is painful now. This message, however, is false. God loves and sees you for who you truly are, freeing you from striving to prove you are unique to get the attention you long for. He rescues you from loneliness, sorrow, and grief. He has given you the most significant identity as his Beloved Child.

Parenting Struggles and Relationship Issues

- You can be self-absorbed and uninterested in your family's feelings or problems due to feeling overwhelmed by your own emotions. Children naturally blame themselves when their parents are struggling, and your moods can make your children feel like they've done something wrong or you don't want to know or help them.

- You may place great expectations on your partner and children for nurturing and support. You can idealize your family, then feel disappointed when they don't live up to that ideal. Even if you don't voice your disappointment, your children can sense they are not living up to your dreams. They can try harder to please you and lose their identity or struggle with self-esteem.

- You can be moody and temperamental, making your children "walk on eggshells." You're also easily wounded by criticism or feedback. As a result, your children will hide their true feelings from you, and you'll miss out on the opportunity to learn from them.

- You may become annoyed when your family tries to cheer you up. Melancholy is like the sweet sadness of your soul and comforts you. It is how you experience the depth of life. But sitting in your sadness causes frustration and confusion for your children. They don't understand why you don't want to be happy and have fun with them. It's important to limit the time you spend in your emotions so you can reconnect and reassure your children.

- You can feel like you're too much and not enough, discounting all your positive attributes as a mother (even the compliments your children give you). Instead, you absorb your negative thoughts, which causes you to struggle to distinguish between reality and fantasy because it all feels real. You perpetually see your weakness and never your glory. As a result, all your incredible and unique giftings are hidden beneath a cloud of negative emotions rather than being used to bless your family.

4

Communication Style

As parents, we can unknowingly look down on our children as lesser beings. Yes, we are older and wiser, and our children are not fully mature, but they are still human beings uniquely created by God. So when it comes to communication, be mindful of your tone, which can be moody or detached if you're not doing well. Treat your children with respect, tenderness, and kindness, acknowledging their growth, level of maturity, and unique personality type. Aim to speak to your children when you are more self-aware, self-regulated, and able to attune to them and their needs. Of course, there will be bad days when you're far from that target and deep in your unhealthy communication style. Instead of falling into blame or shame, embrace grace and take the opportunity to apologize and repair.

When You're Not Doing Well

Your emotional intensity can become reactive. You'll feel as if no one else has ever felt what you're feeling, especially at the level you are feeling it. This causes you to withdraw, which can be regarded as cold and condescending to others. When you finally share your emotions, you steer conversations to focus on what is happening inside you, discounting the experience and feelings of your family. When you find yourself in this unhealthy communication style, take a few deep breaths and let your body relax so your child sees that you have physically softened toward them. Remind yourself that you are God's Beloved Child, and so is your child. From this new place of awareness, you can apologize for your moods and explain to your child that your big feelings are not their fault. Going forward, you can remind yourself that your emotions don't define you, and you can find and experience emotional balance.

When You're Healthy

Your communication style is authentic, deep, and empathetic. You express your feelings with inner balance, modeling a mature acceptance of the full range of human emotions. You are a great listener and can hold your children's big feelings when they are sad or suffering. They can confidently explore and find their place in the world because you appreciate and celebrate their individuality. When your children make mistakes and stumble, as all people do, they know they can count on you to validate their emotions and offer solace and support.

Steps Toward Parenting Growth

- Realize that when your family members don't understand you, it's not necessarily because they don't care.
  - You may be raising children who naturally use their intellect or gut instincts, not their heart, to understand their world. Stay connected and curious so you can learn from one another and become more rounded individuals.
- Mirror other people's moods and conversations back to them instead of focusing on your own feelings. Just like you, your children want to be understood and seen, and because you're not afraid of big emotions, you can comfort them.
  - Often, our children need hugs and our presence more than words: "I can see you're feeling upset right now. I'm here for you and ready to listen if you want to talk. If you're not ready, that's fine too. I'd love to sit next to you if that's okay."
- Be patient when your children express their emotions more slowly than you do. Remember, your children are often dys-regulated by their feelings and don't have the maturity or vocabulary to understand them fully.
  - Keep the focus on them by repeating what they say and giving words to their emotions: "It sounds like you're afraid of losing your friendship, and you don't know how to fix it. Friendships can be hard and confusing sometimes.

4

It's natural to feel this way when your friendships are struggling."

- Display emotional balance. You don't need to feel fewer emotions to work through conflicts, but you must learn to navigate your emotions and stay grounded. When you allow your feelings to pull you into your imagination or false reality, you confuse your children and lose connection.
  - "I'm sorry I've been quiet and moody today. I felt a lot of big, overwhelming emotions, and I let them take me away from you. I want you to know that you did nothing wrong. You are important to me, and I don't want you to think I don't want to be with you. Let's spend some time together. What would you like to do?"
- Recognize that your emotions do not define you. Feelings are transient, and it's natural for them to fluctuate and sometimes overwhelm you.
  - Type 4s often feel like they are their emotions, but your emotions are only a part of you and not the complete picture. Just as you wouldn't define your children by their outbursts or moody days, you shouldn't see yourself as one-dimensional. You possess many unique qualities beyond your emotional depth.
- Embrace mundane aspects of motherhood as opportunities to be a good steward toward your family. The repetitive nature of parenting can feel unfulfilling or uninspiring. You may feel frustrated by the structure and constraints that come with the everyday responsibilities of motherhood. However, routines make life more predictable, which helps your children—who are learning about our big world—feel safe and secure.
  - Honor yourself by finding ways to infuse creativity into your daily routines. Experiment with different approaches or add personal touches that align with your style and

preferences. Discover beauty in the small things by paying attention to the details and nuances of ordinary life. Children are great teachers because they are awed by many things we take for granted.

Your Blind Spot

When you're around those you are most comfortable with (mainly your family), you'll display misaligned characteristics you will not easily recognize. Your family notices, but you are usually blind to them, and that is why we call them blind spots.* Being unaware of your blind spot characteristics can negatively affect your parenting and connection with your children. To become aware of your blind spot, ask yourself the following questions:

- Do I focus on flaws, becoming more judgmental and critical of others and the world?
  - Because you have an idealized version of how things should be, when your children do not meet these ideals, you can become critical and express disappointment. This is especially true if you see your children embodying traits or behaviors that you struggle with and dislike about yourself.
  - Ask yourself, "Am I unfairly imposing my desires and expectations onto my child, and is my criticism truly in their best interest?"
- Am I vocal about my frustrations and disappointments, visibly displaying my disappointment in my body language?

---

* If you're familiar with the Enneagram, you already know that your blind spot displays the average to unhealthy attributes of your Type 1 Path. If you're wondering what Type 1 has to do with Type 4, you can find out more in chapter 28, "Your Enneagram Internal Profile (EIP)."

- It's natural for you to express your emotions authentically. However, you should consider how your words and body language influence your children's emotional well-being.
- Harsh words, dramatic gestures, and critical facial expressions can make your children uneasy. Crossing your arms or avoiding eye contact can create a barrier between you and your child. You can avoid these extremes by breathing deeply. This simple exercise will relax your body, making your body language and your words more welcoming and softer.

• Am I impatient, picky, and controlling when I feel others are incorrect, irresponsible, or not being their authentic selves?
- In your blind spot, you're driven by a desire for a more ideal and authentic world, and you want your family to align quickly with your vision. This controlling behavior can stem from a genuine belief that you know what is right and ideal. You forget that much of life is subjective.
- Finding a balance between honoring your visions and giving your children the freedom to determine their own ideals is essential to building a healthy relationship.

• Am I self-critical, hyperaware of my imperfections, and feeling the need to improve myself to reach what is ideal?
- Outside the house, you feel you need to exaggerate your specialness and uniqueness. However, behind closed doors, you fall into self-deprecation and pressure yourself to obtain your unmet ideals. Most of this happens internally, so you may not think it affects your children. However, children are highly attuned to their mother's moods and use this insight to determine their own security and self-esteem.
- Showing yourself love, compassion, and kindness empowers your children to develop their own sense of worth.

AWARE (Mindfulness Exercise)

Awaken

Awaken to a thought or feeling. It could be:

- The belief that it's not okay to be too much or not enough.
- Feeling envious of someone and like you're missing something vital that they have.
- Feeling unseen or that you don't belong, and that others will never notice how special and unique you are.
- A specific story from your childhood.
- A worry about your parenting, your relationship with your child, or your child's future.
- A feeling of frustration, self-hatred, or shame. (Pay attention to your body. Do your eyes feel teary or sad? Are your shoulders and spine hunched inward? Is there an empty feeling in your gut?)

Welcome

Welcome and extend kindness to this part of you without guilt or shame. Remain curious, not critical. What starts as a thought is connected to a deeper feeling, and what begins as a feeling in your body has a story to share. Stay kind by remembering that this part of you has good intentions. It's trying to help you, even if it's causing you problems.

You can relax knowing that God loves you and sees you for who you truly are—his special and unique creation. He says that you belong as you are, and because of his grace, you can welcome and show kindness to all the parts of your heart.

Ask

Ask God to help you interpret what this part of you is trying to communicate and the motives behind the thoughts and feelings. How is this part of you connected to a wounding story from your childhood?

Resist any urge to drown in your emotions. This can be difficult for Type 4s because you struggle to separate yourself from your feelings. However, just as connecting is the goal for parenting, connecting is also the goal for AWARE. Give this part of your story space to be seen and heard and not swept away by your emotions.

Receive

Receive the forgiveness and compassion God offers you, allowing him to help you guide this misaligned and hurt part of your heart back to the truth. Spend a few minutes reading truths like these verses about your true identity:

- For you created my inmost being; you knit me together in my mother's womb. I praise you because I am fearfully and wonderfully made; your works are wonderful, I know that full well. (Psalm 139:13–14)
- You have searched me, Lord, and you know me. (Psalm 139:1)
- Now you are the body of Christ, and each one of you is a part of it. (1 Corinthians 12:27)

Engage

Engage yourself, your children, and your parenting in a new way, anchored in the truth that you are already complete, delighted in, and fully accepted by God. From this newly aligned place, your children will experience the same support and celebration of their unique identities that you are learning to show yourself.

Prayer for Type 4 Parents

Gracious and loving God, thank you for my unique role as a Type 4 mother. I am grateful for my emotional depth, creativity, and ability to hold my children's complex feelings so I can inspire them to discover their authentic selves. I acknowledge that these qualities reflect your own heart. Thank you for allowing me to demonstrate your love to my family.

I recognize that my desire for the ideal reflects you. At the same time, I acknowledge that my desires can become misaligned and harmful. Thank you for satisfying my core longing to be seen and loved for my specialness and uniqueness. Thank you for making me whole and ensuring I always belong.

Make me aware of my autopilot reactions that do not serve my children well so I can change how I engage with them. I confess my tendencies toward self-absorption, sometimes drowning in my feelings or using my moodiness to manipulate my family's attention. I know my emotional imbalance can overwhelm my children or overshadow their needs. Help me find beauty in the daily responsibilities and routines my children need to feel a sense of stability and security. Keep me engaged and attuned to my children so I don't get lost in my emotional world.

As I guide my children through life's journey, let me be a source of inspiration, encouraging them to explore the depths of their emotions and discover their beauty within. Help me embrace their passions, creativity, and individuality, even when they don't align with my ideals. Forgive me for the times I've not respected my children by expecting them to embody the ideal I have for them. May my children always feel seen by me and loved for their special and unique selves.

In moments of envy, self-doubt, and comparison, remind me of my many gifts. Help me release the pressure to prove that I am special and unique. Keep me grounded so I don't waste time searching for what is missing to become the ideal mother I have created in my head. Help me set boundaries around things like social media, which trigger my envy and lead to unrealistic comparisons. As your Beloved Child, I know I am complete.

Please grow my community so I may find support, encouragement, and a sense of belonging in my parenting journey. Grant me the courage to connect with others even when I'm afraid I won't belong. Surround me with authentic, imperfect, and gracious mothers who appreciate my unique approach to parenting and aren't afraid to go deep with me and explore the vast emotions and struggles that come with motherhood.

As I vulnerably embrace my story and the wounded parts of my heart, help me parent my children from a place of new awareness and emotional groundedness. Fill me with the desire to repair so I can connect deeply with my children and be sensitive to their needs and emotions. As I navigate the joys and challenges of parenting, grant me the gifts of self-love, significance, and belonging. Amen.

CHAPTER 21

Type 5: The Analytical Investigator

Perceptive | Insightful | Intelligent |
Rational | Self-sufficient | Detached

Parenting Core Motivations

Your **Core Fear** is being thought of as an incapable or ignorant mother, being annihilated, invaded, having obligations placed upon you, and having your energy depleted by the demands of motherhood.

Your **Core Desire** is to be a knowledgeable, capable, and competent mother.

Your **Core Weakness** is avarice—feeling you lack inner resources and that too much interaction with others (including your children) will lead to catastrophic depletion.

Your **Core Longing** is to hear and believe that "your needs are not a problem." You feel you will run out of resources you need to survive, but God knows specifically what your needs are and meets them. You can confidently parent from a place of replenishment, not scarcity.

Primary Parenting Perspective

To achieve your core motivations, your primary focus is obtaining more knowledge so you can experience security and independence. You desire this because you perceive the world and people as intrusive, overwhelming, and draining of your already-limited energy reserves.

To preserve your resources, you withdraw from people (including your children) and detach from your emotions until you can recharge alone. Without solitude, you fear you will experience catastrophic depletion.

Parenting on Autopilot

The autopilot response of all parents is to guide their children to become little versions of their type's personality, because it's easier to parent a child to be just like you! Becoming aware of this tendency is a big step toward changing course and parenting with awareness so that you can respect your children's unique personalities and valid perspectives.

As a Type 5, you want to raise "Little Analytical Investigators," children who embody independence, curiosity, intellectual pursuit, and giftedness. You encourage your children to become little geniuses, fostering their love for learning and empowering them to delve into the wonders of the world. You inspire your children to be inquisitive thinkers, always seeking new knowledge and exploring the vast realms of information. You envision your kids as self-reliant.

While these are great qualities to teach your children, when parenting on autopilot, you may expect a level of independence and emotional stability that is inconsistent with their developmental abilities. Most of our children's actions and reactions come from unregulated emotions. By nature, they depend on their caregivers to meet their needs and help them hold their overwhelming feelings. Furthermore, not all personalities value alone time or need to recharge as often as Type 5s. Knowing this can help you step back, parent with curiosity and grace, and allow your children to embrace their unique personalities as they develop more independence and determine their interests.

Parenting Style

You parent with wisdom and curiosity and don't allow your emotions to overtake you, which creates a calm, secure home environment.

You're objective, practical, and make wise decisions for your family based on reason and knowledge. You're interested in the world and observe what others do not notice, offering your children tremendous insight and understanding. You can deconstruct obstacles in your children's way by seeing things from a new perspective and helping them move forward.

However, you feel you lack inner resources and that too much interaction with others (including your children) will deplete your energy reserves. Therefore, you isolate yourself, hold on to your resources, and minimize your needs. To others, your firm boundaries and need for privacy might come across as impersonal, but they are vital for processing and recharging your energy levels. Once renewed, you can reconnect with people again.

The work of parenting requires energy, which can trigger your core weakness of avarice. To better understand yourself as a Type 5, imagine a cell phone battery. Extroverts have an extra interactive battery case that activates when they are out with people, giving them a battery life of 200 percent. Introverts are like cell phones without extra interactive battery power. They start the day fully charged at 100 percent but need some alone time to recharge at the end of the day. However, as a Type 5, your battery level feels more like 40 to 50 percent when you wake up. This means you must carefully discern and ration your energy reserves, as any intrusions or obligations placed on you can quickly deplete your energy. To preserve your energy, you set strict boundaries because you're uncertain when you'll have the opportunity to recharge.

Despite your insatiable thirst for thinking and knowing, you experience the world as an intrusive and overwhelming place. Feeling that life (and motherhood) demands too much of you, you focus on conserving your energy and resources to avoid a sense of catastrophic depletion. This intense desire to hoard and control your environment can damage your relationships because you can be extremely private, stingy, and emotionally distant, even with your children.

5

When you learn to take your struggles and longings to God, you can begin to discover that your needs are not a problem. You know it is good and healthy to recharge your inner battery, and you do so in ways that don't jeopardize your relationships. Restored and renewed, you can give yourself to your family more generously and live not just from your head but also your heart. Then your wise and curious nature can bring out the best in everyone, changing your family tree and making your home (and the world) a better place.

Levels of Alignment: Assessing Your Inner Well-Being

Aligned

Living in this healthy state, you find assurance that God will replenish your depleted reserves and provide for all your needs. Your profound connection with your family empowers you to share your knowledge and insights, assisting others with your wisdom. You observe hidden details and perceive the world through a unique lens, inspiring your children to see life in new and imaginative ways. You are more self-confident, decisive, and physically active, connecting your intellect with your emotions and gut instincts.

Misaligned

Living in this autopilot state, you believe you must supply all your needs. You set firm boundaries to protect yourself from your children becoming too invasive. You fear you will be rejected if you share your needs with your family. So you withdraw from them, detach from your emotions, and protect your inner resources to avoid feeling catastrophic depletion. All of this causes disconnection and can harm your child's attachment to you.

Out of Alignment

Living in this unhealthy state, you are very isolated, hoard your resources, and let your mind veer off and become frightened by your own deep and conspiratorial thinking. You may fear others are planning to harm you, so you reject the parenting support you need to recharge. Lost in your thoughts, you are detached from reality and thus detached from your family. Your children feel emotionally abandoned and, over time, fail to be able to acknowledge and process their own emotions or trust their gut instincts.

Childhood Message

As a child, you were incredibly observant, imaginative, and curious. You loved learning as many things as possible. You grew up believing that the world is intrusive, and you felt extremely embarrassed if you did not know the answers or how to operate in the world. Because the world and relationships were so overwhelming, you desired to be alone most of the time. You needed your parents to honor your need for privacy, space, and time to process your thoughts, feelings, and the day's events, but it was difficult for you to share your inner world, and you often felt rejected by your parents. You felt your needs were too much for others, so you held on to resources to minimize your needs.

Your childhood message is, "It's not okay to be comfortable in the world." This was directly said to you or is a message you perceived through interactions with others. It is hardwired in your mind, like a record player that constantly played when you were a child and continues to play into adulthood. It was painful then, and it is painful now. This message, however, is false. It is okay for you to need extra time alone to recharge. God is the Living Water that does not run dry, so you can go to him for complete renewal. Resting in the truth that you are God's Beloved Child, you can let go of the belief that you must be self-sufficient and can purposely reconnect with your family and the parenting community, allowing them to care for and support you as you give generously to them in return.

Parenting Struggles and Relationship Issues

- You frequently feel intruded upon and need a great deal of privacy. To avoid feeling overwhelmed, you distance yourself from what you believe is draining you: interaction with people and the world. This strategy gives the illusion of being effective since it allows you to restore your energy reserves. But to your children, it can feel like you are ignoring, rejecting, or not being attuned to them.

- You can accumulate a wide range of information, including parenting books and podcasts. You enjoy the idea of motherhood, but not necessarily the practice of motherhood, because parenting is unpredictable and resources are not guaranteed to work. This can leave you dissatisfied, drained, and feeling like a failure.

- When your children come to you with problems, your response can feel cold and data-driven because you intellectualize problems to find solutions. But often, people are not looking for an answer. They want connection and to be seen and heard. And not all personalities prioritize knowledge in the same way you do. Your children may naturally lean more into their gut or emotions.

- You may find yourself easily overwhelmed by the emotional needs of others, especially when it comes to your children, who often experience intense and dysregulated emotions. They rely on you to hold and reflect their big feelings. However, your typical flat affect and lack of emotional display can lead to mis-understandings and disconnection.

- You present yourself as undemanding and as though you don't have needs, including the need for relationships. But as you downplay your need for connection and avoiding social situations, your children also miss out on possible friendships and, later in life, may struggle to form their own relationships.

Communication Style

As parents, we can unknowingly look down on our children as lesser beings. Yes, we are older and wiser, and our children are not fully mature, but they are still human beings uniquely created by God. So when it comes to communication, be mindful of ways you might be talking down to them. Treat your children with respect, tenderness, and kindness, acknowledging their growth, level of maturity, and unique personality type. Aim to speak to your children when you are more self-aware, self-regulated, and able to attune to them and their needs. Of course, there will be bad days when you're far from that target and deep in your unhealthy communication style. Instead of falling into blame or shame, embrace grace and take the opportunity to apologize and repair.

When You're Not Doing Well

You can speak to your children in an overly brief, cold, and intellectually arrogant way. You may tend to talk more about your interests than your child's interests, and you can prioritize teaching them facts and information over emotional intelligence. You might withdraw or emotionally detach when you feel too many relational or parenting obligations placed on you. Because you usually refrain from discussing your needs, your children wonder if they caused you to withdraw (remember, children naturally blame themselves). When you find yourself in this unhealthy communication style, take a few deep breaths and let your body relax so your child sees that you have physically softened toward them. Remind yourself that you are God's Beloved Child, and so is your child. From this new place of awareness, you can begin to ask curious questions about your child's emotions and unique interests and reconnect with them. Going forward, you can remind yourself that God will renew and recharge you, which gives you the energy to connect emotionally with your children, empathize with their feelings, and become a safe place for them to turn to.

When You're Healthy

Your communication style assures your children that your relationship is secure and connected. Your children know you'll always be respectful, nonintrusive, and curious about their thoughts and emotions. You communicate your needs, giving your children context and assurance when you need to withdraw and recharge. As a result, they feel supported, safe, and free to be themselves and dive into their unique interests. When your children make mistakes and stumble, as all people do, they know they can count on your deep well of knowledge and emotional stability to help them find their way forward.

Steps Toward Parenting Growth

- Express your feelings, not just your thoughts and observations, and be curious about your child's emotions.
  - "I'm sorry I've been short with you. I feel overwhelmed by all we have to do today. When I'm like this, how does it make you feel? You can be honest with me. I want to do better and make our busy days more enjoyable."
- Gently communicate your need to process your thoughts and

feelings alone so you can recharge and reengage with your children with more energy.

- "Wow. A lot happened today. Mommy needs some time alone to think and recharge her battery. Just like your tablet needs to be plugged in to keep working, sometimes mommies need to recharge too. I'm going to go to my room to rest. I set out something for you to do while I'm gone, and I'll start a timer so you know when I'll be back. Then we'll do something fun together."

- Learn to read nonverbal cues. People use their body language a great deal when communicating. By watching your child's body language, you can help them see and put words to their competing emotions, helping them connect to their inner world and to you.

- "I noticed your arms are crossed and your face looks sad (mirror your child's expression back to them). I think you're feeling sad and angry because of the fight you had with your brother. It's sometimes confusing to feel two emotions at once. Which emotion feels bigger right now?"

- Allow yourself to need others and express your needs and emotions to trusted adults.

- When you insist on being completely independent, you are distracted and overwhelmed by your needs. The more you allow people to care for you, the more you will feel recharged and available to reengage with your family.

- Don't expect more intellectual achievement than is developmentally possible for your kids, and recognize that not all personalities prioritize knowledge.

- You can overemphasize intellectual growth in your children to prepare them for life's challenges, hoping they will feel more confident than you did as a child. However, if you expect too much too soon, your efforts can have the

5

opposite effect and put undue pressure on your children, leading to stress and anxiety. Your children may be more geared toward athletics, creative arts, socializing, and so on. Use your natural curiosity to learn more about your child's interests and be open to learning from your child. They may introduce you to new ideas, perspectives, or activities you haven't encountered before.

- Assert yourself confidently in your role as your child's mother.
  - There will always be more you can learn about parenting, but if you spend all your time preoccupied with theory, you'll miss experiencing the joys and challenges of parenting in real time. God gave you your children; you're the right person for the job. You can confidently lean into your instincts, emotions, and the knowledge you already possess to parent well in each moment.

Your Blind Spot

When you're around those you are most comfortable with (mainly your family), you'll display misaligned characteristics you will not easily recognize. Your family notices, but you are usually blind to them, which is why we call them blind spots.* Being unaware of your blind spot characteristics can negatively affect your parenting and connection with your children. To become aware of your blind spot, ask yourself the following questions:

- Do I assert my boundaries forcefully and confront anyone who displeases me?

---

* If you're familiar with the Enneagram, you already know that your blind spot displays the average to unhealthy attributes of your Type 8 Path. If you're wondering what Type 8 has to do with Type 5, you can find out more in chapter 28, "Your Enneagram Internal Profile (EIP)."

– Outside the home, you maintain a low profile to avoid conflict, but you can challenge your family members when they displease you or cross your boundaries at home. In your blind spot, you're more willing to engage in debates or confrontations to defend your position, and you draw clear lines regarding what you will tolerate and what is unacceptable.

• Do I become more private and secretive, fearing that others will betray me?

– As a child, you felt your needs were too much for your parents, and no one respected or understood your need for privacy. In your blind spot, you may worry that being vulnerable with your partner and children could lead to dependency or disappointment if your needs are again unmet or your boundaries are not respected.

• Do I question others' competence while asserting my knowledge with strength and intellectual arrogance?

– In your blind spot, you can make your family members and friends feel incompetent and not respected. This can create competitiveness, a lack of teamwork, and emotional distance, which hinder your ability to form and maintain meaningful relationships.

• Do I interrupt conversations with my thoughts and opinions, placing my voice and expertise over others?

– A clear sign you are in your blind spot is when you notice yourself interrupting others, dominating conversations, and rejecting nuance.

– For your children, this signals that their thoughts, feelings, and opinions are not valued, which may lead to frustration, diminished self-esteem, and a lack of confidence in expressing themselves in the future. You also miss learning more about others' interests, concerns, and lived experiences.

AWARE (Mindfulness Exercise)

Awaken

Awaken to a thought or feeling. It could be:

- The belief that it's not okay to be comfortable in the world.
- Feeling anxious that you must gain more information or resources before moving forward.
- Feeling a need to cling to and hoard your time and resources, fearing that generously giving of yourself and resources will lead to catastrophic depletion.
- A specific story from your childhood.
- A worry about your parenting, your relationship with your child, or your child's future.
- A feeling of frustration, overwhelm, or incompetence. (Pay attention to your body. Are your muscles tight and controlled? Do you feel expressionless or flat? Are only your eyes connecting to the world as you observe?)

Welcome

Welcome and extend kindness to this part of you without guilt or shame. Remain curious, not critical. What starts as a thought is connected to a deeper feeling, and what begins as a feeling in your body has a story to share. Stay kind by remembering that this part of you has good intentions. It's trying to help you, even if it's causing you problems.

You can relax knowing that God freely gives you all the knowledge, energy, and resources you need. He welcomes your needs, and because of his grace, you can welcome and show kindness to all the parts of your heart.

Ask

Ask God to help you interpret what this part of you is trying to communicate and the motives behind the thoughts and feelings. How is this part of you connected to a wounding story from your childhood? Resist any urge to overanalyze and intellectualize this part of you. This can be difficult for Type 5s because you struggle to connect to your heart and emotions. However, just as connecting is the goal for parenting, connecting is also the goal for AWARE. Give this part of your story space to be seen, heard, and felt.

Receive

Receive the forgiveness and compassion God offers you, allowing him to help you guide this misaligned and hurt part of your heart back to the truth. Spend a few minutes reading truths like these verses about how God delights in meeting your needs and renewing your mind, body, and soul:

- But those who hope in the LORD will renew their strength. They will soar on wings like eagles; they will run and not grow weary, they will walk and not be faint. (Isaiah 40:31)
- For the LORD gives wisdom; from his mouth comes knowledge and understanding. (Proverbs 2:6)
- "Come to me, all you who are weary and burdened, and I will give you rest." (Matthew 11:28)

Engage

Engage yourself, your children, and your parenting in a new way, from a heart resting in the truth that God sees, understands, and takes care of all your needs. From this newly aligned place, you can generously share the overflow of your wisdom and resources, and your children will experience the same emotional acceptance that you are learning to show yourself.

Prayer for Type 5 Parents

Gracious and loving God, thank you for my unique role as a Type 5 mother. I am grateful for my natural curiosity, valuable insights, and ability to make wise decisions for my family. I acknowledge that these qualities reflect your own heart. Thank you for allowing me to demonstrate your intelligence and wonder.

I recognize that my thirst for knowledge and desire to understand the world reflect you. At the same time, I acknowledge that in a fallen world, my intellectual pursuits can become misaligned and harmful, especially when I withdraw too often from my family. Forgive me for the times I haven't been present and attentive to my children's emotional and physical needs. Thank you for satisfying my core longing to know that my needs are not a problem, so I can ask for and receive help.

Guide me as I set healthy boundaries for myself and my children. May these boundaries foster a sense of safety and security in our family and not become a source of disconnection. Help me find moments of rest and solitude to recharge my mind and spirit, knowing that self-care is essential to properly care for my family. And give me the discernment to know when I need to intentionally reconnect, trusting that doing so will provide me with all the energy and resources I need to stay present and engaged with my family.

Make me aware of my autopilot reactions that do not serve my children well so I can change how I engage with them. Teach me to actively listen to my children's thoughts and feelings with an open heart and mind. Help me model humility, acknowledging that learning is a lifelong journey, and that I do not have all the answers. May I grow and learn alongside my children, share their joys and challenges, and create an environment where they feel heard, valued, and respected. Help me be a source of encouragement, stability, and inspiration as they discover their interests, opinions, and place in the world.

Remind me that I do not walk this path alone. You are with me every step of the way. Thank you for giving me all I need to parent my unique children. *Even though parenting is unpredictable, I can confidently move forward, trusting that you will provide the wisdom and resources I need in each moment.*

Please grow my community so I may find support, encouragement, and a sense of belonging in my parenting journey. I know my children need connection as much as I do, so give me the courage to connect with other families even though I fear depletion. Surround me with authentic, imperfect, and gracious mothers who appreciate how I see the world, respect my boundaries, and help me connect to my emotions.

As I vulnerably embrace my story and the wounded parts of my heart, help me parent my children from a place of new awareness. Fill me with confidence in my abilities, intellectual humility, and the desire to connect and repair. And keep my heart open to the immeasurable impact of emotional intelligence. As I navigate the joys and challenges of parenting, grant me the gifts of rest, renewal, and deep connection. Amen.

5

CHAPTER 22

Type 6: The Faithful Guardian

Committed | Responsible | Faithful |
Vigilant | Suspicious | Anxious

Parenting Core Motivations

Your **Core Fear** is feeling fear itself, not having parenting support, security, or guidance, and being blamed, targeted, alone, or physically abandoned (by support systems or your family).

Your **Core Desire** is to have security, guidance, and support in your parenting journey.

Your **Core Weakness** is anxiety—scanning the horizon of life and trying to predict and prevent negative outcomes (especially worst-case scenarios) and remaining in a constant state of apprehension and worry about your children and your parenting.

Your **Core Longing** is to hear and believe that "you are safe and secure." You feel that you alone can see and prevent dangers, but God says you are not abandoned or alone, and he gives you true peace, rest, assurance, and guidance to parent from a place of confidence.

Primary Parenting Perspective

To achieve your core motivations, your primary focus is predicting and planning for all possible outcomes so you can prevent potential harm from occurring to you and your family. You believe the world is dangerous and that most people have hidden agendas, so you rehearse in your mind what might happen, developing strategies to stop negative circumstances with the goal of keeping yourself and others safe and secure.

Parenting on Autopilot

The autopilot response of all parents is to guide their children to become little versions of their type's personality, because it's easier to parent a child to be just like you! Becoming aware of this tendency is a big step toward changing course and parenting with awareness so that you can respect your children's unique personalities and valid perspectives.

As a Type 6, you want to raise "Little Faithful Guardians." You want your children to embody reliability, obedience, resilience, and trustworthiness. You prioritize building a strong sense of loyalty and commitment in your children, teaching them to be steadfast supporters who remain by the side of their loved ones during challenging times. You help your kids learn to counteract the many uncertainties in the world with extra due diligence and sometimes even wit or humor. You encourage your children to scan the horizon to be prepared for whatever comes their way. You envision them staying safe and keeping others safe.

While these are great qualities to teach your children, when parenting on autopilot, you may expect a level of responsibility and future thinking inconsistent with their developmental abilities. Most of our children's actions and reactions come from unregulated emotions, so they cannot always think critically about the potential consequences of their actions. Furthermore, not all personalities are as cautious, rule-following, or teamwork-oriented as Type 6s. Knowing this can help you step back, parent with curiosity and grace, and allow your children to embrace their unique personalities as they learn to trust their inner guidance and find their place in the world.

Parenting Style

You are reliable, hardworking, dutiful, and steady. You have a great sense of humor and an amazing ability to foresee and solve problems. You are fiercely loyal to your family and are a natural team player. Your children can count on you to remain calm and competent in a crisis and lighten the tension with your wit. (Sometimes laughter is the best medicine.) You prepare your children to be more confident and secure in the world, able to handle life's surprises better than you did growing up.

However, you have an "internal committee" of voices constantly chiming in with contradictory thoughts, various possibilities, analyses, and questions. This inner committee continually causes you to second-guess your parenting, doubt your knowledge, and consult others for advice. You're often plagued by fear, uncertainty, and catastrophic thinking, and you experience the world as a dangerous place where you must be hypervigilant and scan for what could happen because a threat could come from any angle. You try to manage your anxiety by preemptively running all the worst-case scenarios in your mind to plan and predict what could happen.

The work of parenting causes your inner committee to constantly ask, *Well, what about this? Did you think of that?* This can trigger your core weakness of anxiety, leaving you utterly paralyzed. It's extremely hard for you to relax and be present with your children because your mind is constantly spinning, trying to figure out what to do next to ensure everything is okay. Even if you don't say your fears out loud, your children can pick up on your anxiety and begin to believe they are unsafe in the world, preventing them from exploring and stepping out of their comfort zones. If you don't balance safety with encouraging independence and healthy risk-taking, your overprotective nature can cause your children to develop anxiety, low self-esteem, and poor coping skills.

Despite all this, you have tremendous courage and bravery

because you have all the reasons in the world to back down, run away, or be scared. Your inner committee tells you everything that could go wrong, but you move forward faithfully because your family is counting on you, and you want to provide them security. Your children know you are loyal to them and will persevere with them to the end.

When you learn to take your struggles and longings to God, you can begin to let go of your reliance on outside sources to confirm your parenting decisions and philosophy. You can parent with curiosity, courage, and faith, honoring your children's unique personalities and connecting deeply with them. Then your attentive nature can bring out the best in everyone, changing your family tree and making your home (and the world) a better place.

Levels of Alignment: Assessing Your Inner Well-Being

Aligned

Living in this healthy state, you let go of the need to constantly predict and control your life, which allows your mind to calm down and be fully present in each moment. You recognize that earthly safety and security are never guaranteed, yet still trust that God guides you and your children's steps. Learning to trust yourself and your inner discernment becomes essential as you move forward with courage and bravery, knowing that God's love and care for you and your children surpass your own.

Misaligned

Living in this autopilot state, you are constantly vigilant, scanning your horizon for dangers and trying to predict the future. You look outside yourself for dependable authority figures to trust (parents you know or well-known parenting books/platforms). However, you also

6

test these "experts" to see if they really deserve your loyalty and commitment. You become controlling of your family because you believe no one else is as cautious or vigilant as you are, and it is up to you to ensure they are safe and secure.

Out of Alignment

Living in this unhealthy state, you allow your inner committee to rule your heart. Believing all your fears are true, you are hypervigilant and suspicious of everyone. This prevents you and your children from experiencing support and connection from a healthy community. In your downward spiral of anxiety, uncertainty, and chaos, you express all your fears aloud, pulling your children into your spiral and causing them to doubt themselves and see the world as only dangerous.

Childhood Message

As a child, you were cautious, loyal, responsible, and a rule-follower. There were also times you questioned or even rebelled against your authority figures. You believed the world was dangerous and unreliable, so you learned to predict, strategize, and plan what could go wrong to avoid potential harm, chaos, or insecurity. Your "inner committee" started at an early age, informing you of every possible outcome to ensure your safety and security. This inner committee brought uncertainty by creating self-doubt in your decision-making, so you sought clear and reliable guidance from trusted authority figures to help you feel safe and secure. But even then, you sometimes doubted their advice.

Your childhood message is, "It's not okay to trust yourself." This was either directly said to you or is a message you perceived through interactions with others. It is hardwired in your mind, like a record player that constantly played when you were a child and continues to play into adulthood. It was painful then, and it is painful now. This message, however, is false. You are not abandoned or alone because God is with you always, giving you true peace, rest, and guidance. You can have faith that he will provide you with the wisdom, confidence, and courage you need in each moment because you are his Beloved Child.

Parenting Struggles and Relationship Issues

- You can have blind loyalty toward the people you turn to for advice. This can include people you know or authority figures you follow, such as spiritual leaders, authors, or influencers. You struggle to see their flaws or how their parenting advice may not fit your family and their unique needs. Your children may feel controlled, unseen, or like they are failing to live up to your standards, which are actually someone else's standards you've adopted. Ultimately, you keep running into new problems because there is no perfect parenting system.
- You can confuse your family when your inner committee causes contradictory moods and thoughts. You can freeze up when you are anxious or when openly venting your concerns. You can fluctuate between being timid and dependent (phobic) or assertive and rebellious (counterphobic). This confuses your children because they don't know what to expect, which is counterintuitive to the stability you try to provide.
- You can be suspicious of others' intentions and fracture relationships within your community, preventing you and your children from having the relationships and support you long for. You also test others (including your children) to see if they will stay committed, supportive, and loyal to you.

- You fear being targeted, blamed, or accused unfairly, and you have difficulty admitting when you're wrong. This makes it difficult to repair with your children when you are in conflict. When you default to defending yourself, your children learn not to take responsibility for their mistakes.
- You tend to project your thoughts and feelings onto other people. *Projection* is when a person unconsciously attributes their own unwanted thoughts, feelings, and characteristics onto others. Some examples of this in parenting may include:
  - Projecting your insecurities or worries onto your children, which can lead them to become overly concerned about potential dangers.
  - Projecting your fears of abandonment onto your child's social interactions, which can lead them to begin over-anticipating possible rejection.
  - Projecting your uncertainty and doubt about decision-making onto your children, which can lead them to start over-questioning themselves.

Communication Style

As parents, we unknowingly look down on our children as lesser beings. Yes, we are older and wiser, and our children are not fully mature, but they are still human beings uniquely created by God. So when it comes to communication, be mindful of your inner committee, which causes you to be anxious, skeptical, and overly reactive. Treat your children with respect, tenderness, and kindness, acknowledging their growth, level of maturity, and unique personality type. Aim to speak to your children when you are more self-aware, self-regulated, and able to attune to them and their needs. Of course, there will be bad days when you're far from that target and deep in your unhealthy communication style. Instead of falling into blame or shame, embrace grace and take the opportunity to apologize and repair.

As a Type 6, your communication style can vary greatly based on whether you tend to succumb to your fears and anxieties (phobic) or confront your fears and anxieties (counterphobic). Most people lean one way or the other, but it is a spectrum, and you can fluctuate between the two depending on your circumstances.

When You're Not Doing Well and Are More Phobic

You are noticeably anxious in your communication style. To protect yourself and others, you take a people-pleasing approach and are charming, likable, endearing, obedient, and submissive. You struggle to make decisions, so much of your conversations include worst-case scenarios, expressing your doubts, and asking others what they think you should do. This can make your children anxious because they sense your self-doubt but also look to you for answers and stability. When stressed, you can also question your children's motives or blame them for your predicament.

When You're Not Doing Well and Are More Counterphobic

You are more outspoken, aggressive, and argumentative. You move toward your fear with force and strength, facing your anxieties head-on. You want to handle your problems before they handle you. You look rebellious and tough (like a Type 8), but you still struggle with anxiety and self-doubt. This can make your children anxious because they sense this tension within you. They can also feel rushed or steamrolled as you quickly push forward to "defeat" your fears.

When you find yourself in one of these unhealthy communication styles, take a few deep breaths and let your body relax so your child sees that you have physically softened toward them. Remind

6

yourself that you are God's Beloved Child, and so is your child. From this new place of awareness, you can apologize for your overreactions and explain to your child that your worries are not their fault. Going forward, you can be more mindful of your inner committee and the anxiety it causes so you can be calmer and more optimistic with your children.

When You're Healthy

Your communication style is warm, caring, compassionate, witty, and fun. You are a good listener and engage in a healthy, two-way conversation with your children. You create a safe, relational atmosphere by giving them your support, assurance, and loyalty. When your children make mistakes and stumble, as all people do, they know they can count on you to help them solve their problems and move forward courageously.

Steps Toward Parenting Growth

- Build self-confidence in your intuition and parenting abilities. God chose you to parent your child, and you have unique insights into your child's needs.
  - You can counteract negative self-talk with positive affirmations. And when worry overwhelms you, remind yourself of your strengths and capabilities as a parent, your past wins, and the challenges you have already overcome.
- Embrace flexibility by treating everyone as an equal (including yourself). You don't expect others to always be on edge, scanning the horizon for threats, so don't put all that responsibility on yourself. You also deserve moments of independence, carefree fun, and rest.
  - Likewise, give your children space and flexibility to make

decisions that foster their independence and resilience. Instead of communicating your worry, tell your children: "You can do hard things . . . Take it one step at a time . . . Trust your instincts . . . I believe in you . . . I'm here for you."

- Manage the real source of your anxiety—the contradictory thoughts and worst-case possibilities from your "internal committee."
  - Sit in silence and solitude, even if you have only a few minutes a day. Listen to your inner committee respectfully and acknowledge their worries and concerns. Then weigh all the information and trust God to bring you the clarity, wisdom, and peace to move forward. This will be challenging at first because your mind is always racing, but eventually, you'll learn to quiet your inner committee and feel more confident in your discernment.
- Recognize your projections by noticing when you feel defensive or overly sensitive. When you find yourself reacting strongly to a situation, pause before responding. You might be projecting your own fears, insecurities, or motives onto your family, so be open to considering their viewpoints and feelings without immediately dismissing or discounting them.
  - Ask yourself, "Is this about me?" when you notice yourself making assumptions.
  - Ask your children open-ended questions instead of telling them what you think their motives are or immediately assuming the worst: "I noticed that you're scowling and rolling your eyes at your sister. Can you tell me what's going on? Is anything bothering you? Did something happen that I don't know about?"
- Practice self-compassion. All parents struggle with fears and doubts, and even parenting "experts" make mistakes. When

6

you mess up, the most important thing you can do for your children is show yourself compassion so you don't spiral into shame or blame, then repair the relationship by apologizing and actively listening to them.

— "I'm sorry I blamed you when we were running late. I was actually disappointed in myself for losing track of time. Can you forgive me? How did I make you feel? You can be honest with me. I want to do better next time."

• Realize that not everything is within your control and uncertainties are a natural part of life. This realization is scary, but it can also be freeing. You can trust that God is already in your future, so you can spend less time scanning the horizon and planning for the future and more time being present with your family and savoring the time you have together.

— Notice, we're not asking you to never scan or plan. That's an unrealistic goal. Plus, part of your type's superpower is to see what's ahead and help others prepare for it. The goal is to do it less often and with less anxiety so you can rest and enjoy the little (and big) moments with your children.

Your Blind Spot

When you're around those you are most comfortable with (mainly your family), you'll display misaligned characteristics you will not easily recognize. Your family notices, but you are usually blind to them, and that is why we call them your blind spots.* Being unaware of your blind spot characteristics can negatively affect your parenting

---

* If you're familiar with the Enneagram, you already know that your blind spot displays the average to unhealthy attributes of your Type 9 Path. If you're wondering what Type 9 has to do with Type 6, you can find out more in chapter 28, "Your Enneagram Internal Profile (EIP)."

and connection with your children. To become aware of your blind spot, ask yourself the following questions:

- At times, do I deal with fear and stress by shutting down and withdrawing?
  - You're a team player, but when you're at home, you can isolate yourself to handle your struggles alone. You may be trying to protect your children from your emotional reactions, but withdrawing can lead to emotional disconnection because your children naturally blame themselves for your absence. Clearly communicate why you need alone time before disappearing.
  - "Having people over for dinner is so fun, but sometimes I get overwhelmed by all I have to do to prepare for their visit. I feel myself getting grumpy, and I need some time in my room to calm down."
- Do I sometimes forget who I am and what I enjoy because I've chosen security and loyalty to others over my own passions and desires?
  - Feeling like you're in a fog and disconnected from yourself can signal you're in your blind spot. To wake up, engage in practices that promote self-awareness, such as journaling, exercising, connecting with nature, or catching up with longtime friends.
- When overwhelmed, do I stubbornly resist others' demands and use passive-aggressive behaviors to avoid confrontations?
  - Procrastination or resistance can signal that you're in your blind spot. You may find yourself delaying or avoiding tasks when you feel pressured or uncertain of what to do. You'll also use subtle hints or sarcasm to convey your dissatisfaction.
  - When you notice this, step back and see if there is a boundary issue. Sometimes you can be too much of a team player

6

and say yes when you should have said no. Motherhood can max out your mental and physical load, so learning to say no is essential to you and your family's health. Instead of taking one for the team and feeling resentful about it later, communicate your needs and trust that people will understand that sometimes all you can physically do is show up loyally for your family and yourself.

- Do I get irritated when my family disturbs and interrupts my comfortable routines or cozy environment?
  - Your routines give you a sense of security and predictability that helps you manage your anxiety. Any disruption (even from your children) can threaten the stability you're trying to maintain. It can also make you feel like no one sees all the work you do. When you say things like, "Don't you see how hard I work? Why can't you just give me a break?" you're in your blind spot.
  - It's important to have realistic expectations. Some disruptions are inevitable, especially when you have young children. Furthermore, some personalities enjoy unplanned days and surprises, and the best way to honor your family's unique personalities is to find a balance between predictability and flexibility.

AWARE (Mindfulness Exercise)

Awaken

Awaken to a thought or feeling. It could be:

- The belief that it is not okay to trust yourself.
- One of the many concerns from your inner committee.
- A desire to stop this mindfulness practice and plan or prepare for a future need.

- A specific story from your childhood.
- Self-doubt about your parenting abilities and the desire to seek answers or guidance from an "expert."
- A feeling of responsibility, disconnection, or worry. (Pay attention to your body. Is your jaw clenched, or is your body tense? Does your head feel too full, or overwhelmed and foggy? Are your eyes quickly scanning your surroundings?)

Welcome

Welcome and extend kindness to this part of you without guilt or shame. Remain curious, not critical. What starts as a thought is connected to a deeper feeling, and what begins as a feeling in your body has a story to share. Stay kind by remembering that this part of you has good intentions. It's trying to help you, even if it's causing you problems.

You can relax knowing that because of God, you are not alone or abandoned. He welcomes you and says you are safe, and because of his grace, you can welcome and show kindness to all the parts of your heart.

Ask

Ask God to help you interpret what this part of you is trying to communicate and the motives behind the thoughts and feelings. How is this part of you connected to a wounding story from your childhood? Resist any urge to question your intuition. This can be difficult for Type 6s because your inner committee always chimes in with feelings of doubt, fear, and anxiety. However, just as connecting is the goal for parenting, connecting is also the goal for AWARE. Give this part of your story space to be seen and heard.

Receive

Receive the forgiveness and compassion God offers you, allowing him to help you guide this misaligned and hurt part of your heart back to the truth. Spend a few minutes reading truths like these verses about God's guidance and protection:

6

- "Be strong and courageous. Do not be afraid; do not be discouraged, for the LORD your God will be with you wherever you go." (Joshua 1:9)
- God is our refuge and strength, a very present help in trouble. (Psalm 46:1 ESV)
- "Therefore do not worry about tomorrow, for tomorrow will worry about itself." (Matthew 6:34)

Engage

Engage yourself, your children, and your parenting in a new way, resting in the truth that you are not alone or abandoned because the God of the universe is with you always and already in your family's future. From this newly aligned place, your children will experience the same joyful trust you are learning to show yourself.

Prayer for Type 6 Parents

Gracious and loving God, thank you for my unique role as a Type 6 mother. I am grateful for my faithfulness, courage, and ability to help my children troubleshoot their problems and work as a team. I acknowledge that these qualities reflect your own heart. Thank you for allowing me to demonstrate your loyalty and love to my family.

I recognize that my desire for support and security reflects you. At the same time, I acknowledge that my desires can become misaligned and harmful. Forgive me for the times I've blindly given my trust and loyalty to people and systems out of fear. Thank you for being all-powerful, satisfying my core longing to be safe and secure, and giving me clarity and certainty in a confusing and chaotic world.

Help me discern between the doubts of my inner committee and wisdom. Teach me to recognize truth amid the noise of my fears so that I may follow my inner guidance with confidence and clarity. I know you have equipped me with the tools I need to navigate the complexities of mother-hood, so I can humbly explore and trust my intuition and instincts. Thank you for being with me every step of the way.

I desire the ability to embrace each moment's beauty without fear. You hold the future in your hands, so I can stay present with my children and savor each moment. When worry overwhelms my heart, remind me of your promises and unwavering love. Thank you for working everything together for good, and for standing at the horizon so that I don't have to constantly scan it.

Make me aware of my autopilot reactions that do not serve my children well so I can change how I engage with them. Help me balance my need for stability with an openness to the unexpected. Grant me the wisdom to discern when to hold on to routines and when to embrace flexibility for the well-being of my family. I know you created my children with unique personalities, and that you have a plan and purpose for each of their lives. Give me the courage to trust your wisdom and let go of my need to overprotect and control their future.

Please grow my community so I may find support, encouragement, and a sense of belonging in my parenting journey. Give me the courage to connect with others even when I fear abandonment. Surround me with authentic, imperfect, and gracious mothers who appreciate my humor and offer a safe place for me to share my concerns without being judged for my anxiety.

As I vulnerably embrace my story and the wounded parts of my heart, help me parent my children from a place of new awareness so I can be fully present and not worried about what's next. Fill me with the desire to repair our relationship, so I can connect deeply with my children and be sensitive to their unique personalities and emotions. As I navigate the joys and challenges of parenting, grant me the gifts of inner guidance, a restful heart, and a quiet mind. Amen.

CHAPTER 23

Type 7: The Enthusiastic Optimist

Playful | Excitable | Versatile |
Spontaneous | Scattered | Escapist

Parenting Core Motivations

Your **Core Fear** is that you (or your children) will be deprived, trapped in emotional pain, limited, bored, or miss out on something fun.

Your **Core Desire** is to be a happy, fully satisfied, content parent.

Your **Core Weakness** is gluttony—feeling a great emptiness inside and having an insatiable desire to "fill yourself up" with experiences and stimulation.

Your **Core Longing** is to hear and know that "you will be taken care of." You battle anxiety that you will never really get what you want and need and that you will always feel a deep emptiness inside. But God completely fulfilled your needs, so you can savor the present moment with a grateful heart.

Primary Parenting Perspective

To achieve your core motivations, your primary focus is resisting anything that resembles pain, sadness, grief, boredom, negativity, or anxiety, as you believe these feelings may bring you (and your children) great harm. Therefore, you have perfected the art of escaping these experiences by focusing on and pursuing anything new, fun, exciting, entertaining, and stimulating, hoping it will fill your emptiness and bring you and your family satisfaction.

Parenting on Autopilot

The autopilot response of all parents is to guide their children to become little versions of their type's personality, because it's easier to parent a child to be just like you! Becoming aware of this tendency is a big step toward changing course and parenting with awareness so that you can respect your children's unique personalities and valid perspectives.

As a Type 7, you want to raise "Little Enthusiastic Optimists," children who exude energy, positivity, adaptability, and a willingness to embrace new experiences. You foster a love for trying new things and encourage your kids to be young adventurers, spreading happiness and laughter wherever they go. You encourage your children to approach life with a zestful spirit. You envision them always seeking new opportunities for fun and exploration.

While these are great qualities to teach your children, when parenting on autopilot, you can expect a level of positivity and adaptability inconsistent with their developmental abilities. Children often have unregulated emotions and depend on their caregivers to help them hold their overwhelming feelings. These feelings are scary to them and not fun for you. Furthermore, not all personalities have as much energy and love of adventure as Type 7s. Knowing this can help you step back, parent with curiosity and grace, and allow your children to embrace their unique personalities as you provide the structure and downtime they need to flourish.

7

Parenting Style

You parent with optimism and creativity, encouraging your children to pursue their dreams and overcome obstacles. You offer your children hope for the future by seeing endless possibilities and innovation all around you. You are fun, engaging, motivating, and always willing to try something new. As a lover of variety, you live life "big" and remain eager to enjoy and share with your children all the experiences this world offers.

However, though you radiate positivity and happiness on the outside, internally, you always long for more and fear missing out. To you, life is like cotton candy—super sweet to the taste, but it disappears quickly, leaving you constantly unsatisfied and wanting more. You hate to be limited, restricted, or bored, because that's when you feel a deep emptiness inside. When life is hard, you experience an internal struggle to avoid pain at all costs and quickly escape to things that please you.

The work of parenting can be difficult for you because, by nature, it is time-consuming, restrictive, and not always fun, which can trigger your core weakness of gluttony. You'll settle for any stimulation or experience to distract yourself from your anxieties. This can make your children feel second best to your social life and adventures. Children naturally blame themselves when they feel disconnected from a parent. They can't read your mind and don't know that you battle a fear that you will never really get what you want and need.

As you pursue your need for happiness and stimulating experiences, you cannot enjoy the present moment or feel satisfied with what you already have. Your children can feel abandoned and like they're not enough to make you happy. Putting painful things out of your awareness or reframing suffering into something positive without genuinely dealing with it will always show up in counterproductive ways throughout your life. This can negatively affect the depth of your relationship with your family and your children's ability to process their own difficult emotions.

When you learn to take your struggles and longings to God, you can begin to let go of your dissatisfaction. You can slow down, be present with your family, and experience deep gratitude for the life and blessings you already have. Then your joyful and creative nature can bring out the best in everyone, changing your family tree and making your home (and the world) a better place.

Levels of Alignment: Assessing Your Inner Well-Being

Aligned

Living in this healthy state, you stay grounded, see your blessings, and feel gratitude and satisfaction. You remain playful with your children but are also responsible and focused, setting healthy boundaries to balance adventure and rest. Finding contentment in God allows you to experience all your emotions and deal with sadness and disappointment, equipping you to help your children hold and process their own difficult emotions.

Misaligned

Living in this autopilot state, you reject any sadness or disappointment as you create many new, exciting experiences to avoid stress and boredom. This includes avoiding your family when relationships get tough. You also reframe negatives to positives, point out silver linings to a fault, and have difficulty feeling your sadness or tolerating your children's difficult emotions.

Out of Alignment

Living in this unhealthy state, you fear missing out and reject any restrictions and limitations placed on you. You become self-focused and an escapist, willing to take risks that can put you and your family in harm's way. You blame others (including your family) for your dissatisfaction, believing they keep you from joy and happiness. You fail to see your self-sabotage or that your insatiable appetite cannot be quenched with earthly pleasures. Therefore, you keep taking bigger risks, believing you will find what you're looking for. However, this approach only leads to more destruction and dissatisfaction. All the while, you refuse to see the truth, holding on to the belief that everything will turn out great in the end.

7

Childhood Message

As a child, you felt disconnected and emotionally cut off from one or both parents who were supposed to nurture you. Therefore, you determined you couldn't rely on others and needed to nurture and care for yourself, so you focused on obtaining what you needed to be happy, content, and satisfied. When you felt an unpleasant emotion or were bored or deprived, you distracted yourself with things like toys, games, friends, TV, computers, sports, and humor. You used your active mind to create a world full of happy thoughts and exciting adventures so you could flood and neutralize your painful thoughts and feelings.

Your childhood message is, "It's not okay to depend on anyone for anything." This was either directly said to you or is a message you perceived through interactions with others. It is hardwired in your mind, like a record player that constantly played when you were a child and continues to play into adulthood. It was painful then, and it is painful now. This message, however, is false. God provides you with the care and tenderness your heart craves. The relief he offers is all-satisfying and fills the emptiness you feel inside. Filled with his nurturing care and provision, you can stay grounded in the moment, deeply connected to your family as you experience the gratitude and contentment of being God's Beloved Child.

Parenting Struggles and Relationship Issues

- You love a good time and enjoy new experiences, but that high-energy approach that draws people to you can also drive others away. Your children can become exhausted by your nonstop, activity-packed life, and you can become impatient with the slower pace of your family.

- You talk about yourself a lot, and other people can feel they rarely have an opportunity to share about themselves. Relationships can feel self-centered and one-sided. This keeps you from connecting deeper with other mothers, and your children can feel unseen and unappreciated.

- You may avoid difficult conversations, situations, and emotions by becoming an escapist and ignoring anything negative. Similarly, when your children have problems, you distract them from their sadness with fun experiences, food, shopping, and so forth. Your children learn to put a Band-Aid over their pain instead of learning to truly process and understand their emotions.

- You falsely believe that people will not support you if you share your negative emotions and thoughts, so you demand immediate gratification, insist on quick-and-easy solutions to your and your family's problems, and fill your home with constant entertainment. You can struggle to realize that boredom and quiet time are blessings that allow you and your children to rest and experience creative insight and self-discovery.

- By rationalizing your unacceptable thoughts, feelings, and actions, you can avoid owning your real motivations or the ways your behavior affects your family. You are skilled at charming your way out of trouble by spinning any negative situation into one that sounds positive, fun, and exciting. You are so upbeat and likable that it is hard for your family to stay angry or upset with you. This can lead to your children blaming themselves or doubting their own intuition during conflicts.

Communication Style

As parents, we can unknowingly look down on our children as lesser beings. Yes, we are older and wiser, and our children are not fully mature, but they are still human beings uniquely created by God. So when it comes to communication, be mindful of your tendency to focus on yourself and your needs. Treat your children with respect, tenderness, and kindness, acknowledging their growth, level of maturity, and unique personality type. Aim to speak to your children when you are more self-aware, self-regulated, and able to attune to them and their needs. Of course, there will be bad days when you're far from that target and deep in your unhealthy communication style. Instead of falling into blame or shame, embrace grace and take the opportunity to apologize and repair.

When You're Not Doing Well

You can be hyper and scattered. Your children may feel uneasy and exhausted as you rush from one activity to the next, or they may feel second best to your social life. You keep attention on yourself by telling long and grand stories, and your family feels more like spectators than equals. When you or your children experience difficulty or pain, you try to reframe negatives and avoid anything pessimistic or too deep. If that doesn't work, you look for an escape, which can cause your children to feel abandoned or teach them not to share their emotions. When you find yourself in this unhealthy communication style, take a few deep breaths and let your body relax so your child sees that you have physically softened toward them and you're not going anywhere. Remind yourself that you are God's Beloved Child, and so is your child. From this new place of awareness, you invest more deeply in your relationship with your children, helping you both process and accept your emotions.

When You're Healthy

Your communication style is fun, lively, lighthearted, optimistic, and joyful. Your family can relax and have fun with you, trusting that you will balance play with rest, and adventure with structure and predictability. You share the stage and take the time to listen to others without monopolizing the conversation. You remain grounded even in challenging discussions and can feel and express your painful emotions. When your children make mistakes and stumble, as all people do, they know they can count on you not to jump to the silver lining but instead sit with them and help them hold their overwhelming emotions.

Steps Toward Parenting Growth

- Intentionally set priorities and limitations so you are more rested, dependable, and grounded.
  - You may think you're on a great adventure, but you often run in circles. Escaping from your pain feels exciting, but it's also exhausting. When the fun is over, you don't have any energy left to deal with your inner world of emotions, so you run again. Setting and sticking to boundaries will help you (and your children) feel more rested to process your inner world so you can avoid this cycle.
- Listen patiently and remember that not everyone is as quick of a thinker as you are.
  - Practice active listening with your children by asking open-ended questions, repeating what you've heard them say, and embracing moments of silence. Silence is hard for you, but remember to refrain from monopolizing the conversation or trying to get to a resolution too quickly. Your children are slowly figuring out their emotions and how the world operates, so give them time to put words to their feelings and experiences.
- Acknowledge that life and conversations cannot always be fun. Trust that you can work through painful conversations without

7

reframing or escaping. When you make a mistake, try not to put a positive spin on it. Accept your part in the conflict and ask for forgiveness.

- "I'm sorry I wasn't home to help you with your school project. I should have checked in to see what you needed from me before I made plans with my friends. I want to do better next time. Can you share how this made you feel? You can be honest, and I promise to listen without interrupting you."

• Build a strong bond with your children through creativity and collaboration.

- You'll be more present in life when you spend less time looking for ways to consume and more time creating. Parenting offers an opportunity to walk alongside your kids, share ideas, and work together. Utilize your innate creativity to make memorable experiences that showcase both your and your child's unique personalities. When your kids reflect on their lives, they'll see intentional experiences you created together, moments where they felt seen, included, and valued.

• Embrace the parenting process, and don't focus on reaching the end of each stage. Even during challenging phases of parenting, there are beautiful moments you will cherish and yearn for later on.

- Children are great teachers. Let them show you how to become present to the wonders around you. You can do this by observing or playing with them. You can also prompt conversations about your senses: "Tell me what you see/hear/smell/feel."

- Practice gratitude by listing in a journal or on your phone what you love and will miss about your child's current stage of life. Reminding yourself of these little joys will make you more content and motivated to remain engaged with your children instead of looking for an escape or daydreaming about grass that seems greener in the next stage of life.

- Don't just "live" in the moment; "feel" in the moment. When you tolerate only positivity and happiness, you live a one-dimensional life. Model to your children that it's okay to feel a wide range of emotions, including sadness, anger, frustration, or fear, as these emotions are a natural part of being human.
  - "I'm sorry to hear that. It's okay to feel sad sometimes. Tell me more about it."
  - "I understand how that can make you feel angry. It's okay to feel that way. Would some deep breaths help? I'll do them with you."

Your Blind Spot

When you're around those you are most comfortable with (mainly your family), you'll display misaligned characteristics you will not easily recognize. Your family notices, but you are usually blind to them, and that is why we call them blind spots.* Being unaware of your blind spot characteristics can negatively affect your parenting and connection with your children. To become aware of your blind spot, ask yourself the following questions:

- Am I sometimes fiercely independent, building boundaries to protect myself from others being too invasive or limiting my life?

---

* If you're familiar with the Enneagram, you already know that your blind spot displays the average to unhealthy attributes of your Type 5 Path. If you're wondering what Type 5 has to do with Type 7, you can find out more in chapter 28, "Your Enneagram Internal Profile (EIP)."

- When you're in your blind spot, you struggle to trust people and prefer not to be around them. You strongly desire freedom and independence, seeing others (including your family) as too controlling or needy.
- Instead of thinking the worst of people, choose a gracious interpretation when things don't go according to your plans. You'll find that your children aren't trying to limit you. They want to connect with you and be invited into your adventures.

• Do I need to sort out my feelings using my intellect before moving forward?
- In your blind spot, you'll have fewer positive feelings about your life and experience dark and pessimistic viewpoints. Your feelings aren't bad, and you shouldn't hide them from your family, but problems arise when you use only your head to intellectualize a way out of them. Refusing to feel your emotions creates a boomerang effect, causing the same issues to continue popping up. If you truly want to move forward, allow yourself to grieve your pain so that your emotions can be processed and released.

• Do I grow tired of constantly feeling like I need to be positive?
- Out in the world, you're always "on" and entertaining others with your stories. The exhaustion catches up to you at home, and you can feel resentment that others always expect you to be the life of the party. This resentment can leak out and affect your family.
- Be honest about your feelings so your family doesn't have to wonder if they've done something wrong. Everyone needs a break from being the center of attention, so it's okay to seek support and understanding from those closest to you.

• At times, am I secretive or do I isolate myself from others to recharge my internal battery?

- In your blind spot, you conserve your energy by becoming less excitable and more of an observer, and you may withdraw and seek seclusion. Your children can feel disconnected from you, especially if you don't clarify your needs and intentionally reconnect after you've rested. They may also feel like you save all your fun energy for other people.
- If you're constantly pouring yourself out socially and coming home exhausted, that's a sign you're out of balance and need to say no more often.

AWARE (Mindfulness Exercise)

Awaken

Awaken to a thought or feeling. It could be:

- The belief that it's not okay to depend on anyone for anything.
- A desire to reframe a negative into a positive.
- An urge to stop this mindfulness practice and do something fun.
- A specific story from your childhood.
- A worry about your parenting, your relationship with your child, or your child's future.
- A feeling of emptiness, frustration, or sadness. (Pay attention to your body. Are you pacing and having a hard time sitting still? Is your posture tense, or are your fists or jaw clenched? Do you have a heavy, empty feeling in your gut?)

Welcome

Welcome and extend kindness to this part of you without guilt or shame. What starts as a thought is connected to a deeper feeling, and

7

what begins as a feeling in your body has a story to share. Stay kind by remembering that this part of you has good intentions. It's trying to help you, even if it's causing you problems.

You can relax knowing that God says he will fulfill your needs and give you true satisfaction. He provides a calm and safe place to feel your emotions, and because of his grace, you can welcome and show kindness to all the parts of your heart.

Ask

Ask God to help you interpret what this part of you is trying to communicate and the motives behind the thoughts and feelings. How is this part of you connected to a wounding story from your childhood? Resist any urge to flee this exercise. This can be difficult for Type 7s because silence makes you anxious, and your mind always thinks of the next thing you could do. However, just as connecting is the goal for parenting, connecting is also the goal for AWARE. Give this part of your story patience and a quiet space to be seen and heard.

Receive

Receive the forgiveness and compassion God offers you, allowing him to help you guide this misaligned and hurt part of your heart back to the truth. Spend a few minutes reading truths like these verses about God's abundance and care:

- "But whoever drinks of the water that I will give him will never be thirsty again. The water that I will give him will become in him a spring of water welling up to eternal life." (John 4:14 ESV)
- Cast all your anxiety on him because he cares for you. (1 Peter 5:7)
- Satisfy us in the morning with your unfailing love, that we may sing for joy and be glad all our days. (Psalm 90:14)

Engage

Engage yourself, your children, and your parenting in a new way, resting in the truth that God will calm your mind, help you hold your emotions, and fully satisfy your heart. From this newly aligned place, your children will experience the same intentional presence and deep gratitude you are learning to embrace yourself.

Prayer for Type 7 Parents

Gracious and loving God, thank you for my unique role as a Type 7 mother. I am grateful for my optimism, playfulness, and ability to help my children pursue their dreams and overcome obstacles. I acknowledge that these qualities reflect your own heart. Thank you for allowing me to demonstrate your creativity and enthusiasm for my family.

I recognize that my desire for everlasting joy and satisfaction reflects you. At the same time, I acknowledge that my desires can become misaligned and harmful. Forgive me for the times that I've been insensitive to the needs and feelings of my family in my pursuit of pleasure and excitement. Thank you for satisfying my core longing to be taken care of so I don't have to rely on temporary distractions to find fulfillment.

You know the void inside me that longs to be filled. I try to fill myself with material possessions and the excitement of new experiences. Yet, my broken jars cannot hold water for long, and I find myself always searching for more, never fully satisfied with the life I have. This way of living is exhausting and unfulfilling. Please fill me with your stream of living water that never runs dry.**

Guide me as I balance my desire for excitement and new experiences with my responsibilities and my children's needs. Reveal your joy and adventure amid our everyday routines and responsibilities. Teach me to

7

** Jeremiah 2:11–19

be fully present with my children so I can cherish our moments together and feel gratitude for the blessings you've given us.

Make me aware of my autopilot reactions that do not serve my children well so I can change how I engage with them. Fill me with your patience and understanding toward my children's unique personalities and preferred pace of life. As I listen to my children's needs and hold their emotions, let me be a source of comfort and support. Remind me that it's okay to slow down, rest, and to be vulnerable and honest about my own emotions and needs.

Please grow my community so I may find support, encouragement, and a sense of belonging in my parenting journey. Give me the courage to seek help and support when I feel anxious or empty, trusting that it's okay to lean on others. Surround me with authentic, imperfect, and gracious mothers who appreciate my energy and creativity but don't expect me to always be the life of the party.

As I vulnerably embrace my story and the wounded parts of my heart, help me parent my children from a place of new awareness so I can fully savor each moment and not get caught up in what's next. Fill me with the desire to repair our relationship so I can connect deeply with my children and be sensitive to their unique needs. As I navigate the joys and challenges of parenting, grant me the gifts of gratitude, a restful mind, and a satisfied heart. Amen.

CHAPTER 24

Type 8: The Passionate Protector

Assertive | Self-Confident | Intense |
Big-Hearted | Independent | Confrontational

Parenting Core Motivations

Your **Core Fear** is that you (and your children) will be weak, powerless, harmed, controlled, vulnerable, manipulated, and left at the mercy of injustice.

Your **Core Desire** is to protect yourself, your children, and those in your small inner circle.

Your **Core Weakness** is lust/excess—constantly desiring intensity, control, and power, and pushing yourself willfully on life and people (including your family) to get what you want.

Your **Core Longing** is to hear and believe that "you will not be betrayed." You feel you must protect yourself (and your children) against powerlessness and betrayal by having an invincible exterior. But God says he will protect you and never forsake you, so you can reveal your vulnerable heart and parent with tenderness and patience.

Primary Parenting Perspective

To achieve your core motivations, your primary focus is not to be controlled or harmed or to allow others to have any power over you (physical, emotional, or financial). You don't back down when you desire something and can persuasively convince others to give you what you want. You put on an intimidating and strong armor to guard your heart, and your highest priority is protecting yourself and your family from being blindsided, betrayed, or at the mercy of injustice.

Parenting on Autopilot

The autopilot response of all parents is to guide their children to become little versions of their type's personality, because it's easier to parent a child to be just like you! Becoming aware of this tendency is a big step toward changing course and parenting with awareness so that you can respect your children's unique personalities and valid perspectives.

As a Type 8, you want to raise "Little Passionate Protectors," children who embody the qualities of strength, independence, bravery, and resilience. You help your kids learn to stand up for themselves and to stand against injustice as they avoid being wrongly controlled or manipulated by others. You encourage them to develop a strong sense of self-assurance and determination, nurturing them to become young leaders. You envision that your kids will fearlessly take on challenges and bring their ideas to fruition.

While these are great qualities to teach your children, when parenting on autopilot, you may expect a level of independence and toughness inconsistent with their developmental abilities. Most of our children's actions and reactions come from unregulated emotions. By nature, they are dependent on caregivers and have tender hearts. Furthermore, not all personalities are natural leaders or as confident as Type 8s. It's important to be patient and accept your kids' unique temperaments rather than expecting them to be just like you. Knowing this can help you step back, parent with curiosity and grace, and allow your children to embrace their unique personalities as they develop more independence and discover their interests and place in the world.

Parenting Style

You parent with strength, passion, and determination to make things happen. Your children know you will seek justice for them and always protect them. They can trust you to be a decisive and assertive leader who helps them build self-confidence, navigate life's circumstances, and claim their place in this world. You present yourself as a strong, self-assured, and independent mother in the hopes of preventing you and your children from harm or injustice.

However, beneath your layers of armor is a very tender heart. You desire someone bigger and stronger to help carry the load and protect you and your family so you can rest from your role of vigilant protector and remove your heavy armor to reveal your gentle, caring side. Unfortunately, you feel like no one will adequately fill this role and that only you can protect yourself and your children against betrayal and powerlessness by always having an invincible exterior and minimizing personal vulnerability.

The work of parenting can feel very vulnerable, which can trigger your core weakness of lust/excess. You can respond to weakness and vulnerability by being too blunt, confrontational, insensitive, domineering, and cynical, even with your family. While other personalities fear people and become passive, Type 8s fear people and become assertive and even aggressive. Your personality says, "I'll control them before they can control me." While this defense strategy is effective, you don't usually see the negative impact of your energy. However, your children may fear you or withhold information, afraid of how you might react. They can also learn to hide their own vulnerabilities behind thick armor. Inevitably, this self-protection does more harm than good because you miss out on true intimacy and support when you hide your heart.

You can think of Type 8s like snowplows. When there's a lot of snow on the ground, powerful diesel trucks plow a path for others. Likewise, it is inspiring when you make a way for others. We need your strength and willingness to create paths that others cannot create for themselves. However, when you are unhealthy, people on the side of the road or standing in front of your plow can be run over, so you

8

must learn to use your strength for the good of everyone. Likewise, be careful not to overprotect your children because this can cause them to have anxiety, low self-esteem, and poor coping skills. Like with all of life, you need to find a balance. Encouraging independence and healthy risk-taking is just as important as protecting your children.

When you learn to take your struggles and longings to God, you can begin to relax and reveal your softer side, knowing that you have a true Advocate you can trust to stand up for you and protect your family. You can parent with vulnerability and tenderness, understanding that it takes great strength and courage to do so. Then your natural leadership skills can bring out the best in everyone, changing your family tree and making your home (and the world) a better place.

Levels of Alignment: Assessing Your Inner Well-Being

Aligned

Living in this healthy state, you channel your intensity and strength to create a way for those who need support. Instead of fiercely forging ahead, you become open to others' perspectives and feelings as you consider their needs. You let down your tough exterior, showing a tender and gentle side, proving that vulnerability is a mark of courage, and you inspire your children to do the same. Your family trusts you will provide, protect, and champion them with great passion and respect.

Misaligned

Living in this autopilot state, you employ your intensity and confrontational approach to deter perceived threats to you and your family. Unyielding in the face of confrontation, you may disregard others' feelings and be too direct and impatient. You challenge others to reveal the truth, even if it means intimidating them. Blinded by certainty, you won't back down and, like a snowplow, will push others (including your family) out of the way to stay on task, reach your goals, and get what you want or what you think your family needs.

Out of Alignment

Living in this unhealthy state, you are driven by the belief that securing protection and your desired outcomes for yourself and your family is paramount. This mindset propels you to pursue your version of the best path, even if it means trampling others to achieve it. Your intensity can lead to domineering, inconsiderate, and mean-spirited behaviors. You assume everyone has a plan to hurt or control you, prompting you to control others first (including your family). Seeing the world as black and white, you fail to see your children's unique personalities and needs. You believe you know what is best for them and that only you can protect and lead them. You take matters into your own hands, intentionally plow over others, and do whatever it takes to defend yourself and your inner circle.

Childhood Message

As a child, you perceived that the world was aggressive and antagonistic, and only the strong, forceful, and smart survive. You saw how the weak, innocent, and vulnerable were hurt or betrayed. You did not want to be one of these vulnerable people (or you experienced being taken advantage of at an early age), so you decided to protect your heart with strong armor by being assertive, confrontational, dominating, and self-determined. Your heart was so soft and tender that it devastated you when it was exposed and taken advantage of. Wearing protective armor felt necessary for survival. You rarely allowed others to experience your tender side, but it was an amazing experience when you did.

199

Your childhood message is, "It's not okay to be vulnerable or to trust anyone." This was either directly said to you or is a message you perceived through interactions with others. It is hardwired in your mind, like a record player that constantly played when you were a child and continues to play into adulthood. It was painful then, and it is painful now. This message, however, is false. God says that he will never betray you. He is your Good Shepherd who desires to protect and care for you. Resting in this truth, you can let go of the belief that you must always maintain a strong protective front. You can lower your armor and be vulnerable with your children and trusted members of your parenting community, showing up not only as a generous advocate but also as God's Beloved Child.

Parenting Struggles and Relationship Issues

- You struggle with anger that feels like fire in the gut, which must be expelled immediately when ignited. This can cause you to lose your temper, be too blunt, or unleash your powerful intensity, causing your children to be fearful and anxious. Your children might become less likely to share their feelings and concerns when they are unsure of your possible reaction.
- You might begin to believe that others have rejected, betrayed, or disappointed you, so you demand immediate honesty from them. This can be difficult for the person on the receiving end because not all personalities can immediately know what is happening inside them and promptly communicate it. Some individuals need more time to discern their inner experiences. This is especially significant for children who need a supportive adult to help them understand their big feelings and motivations. Nonetheless, the uncertainty of waiting for an answer

can cause you restlessness and the perception that even your children are concealing things.

- You can withdraw from relationships or cut off people if you feel hurt. Your children may carry an emotional burden, wondering if they are responsible for your withdrawal. When you cut off your friends, your children also lose relationships, and you miss out on the opportunity to repair your relationships and receive healthy accountability because you seek advice only from those you currently trust.

- You can be possessive in relationships to maintain a sense of control to protect yourself from potential hurt. You may be jealous of your child's other relationships or activities done without you. You can also be overprotective and not allow your children space to make mistakes and learn from them. Serious issues arise if you use forceful and controlling tactics to change your family into who you want them to be and toward what you want them to do.

- You present a strong exterior and deny the reality that you are human—vulnerable and susceptible to being wrong, harmed, and controlled like everyone else. This denial makes you overly confident in your rightness and invincibility, causing you to make poor decisions that negatively affect your family. You can also refuse to see when you are hurtful or insensitive to others. Your family and friends can feel gaslit, question their intuition, and blame themselves during disagreements because your confidence overpowers them.

Communication Style

8

As parents, we can unknowingly look down on our children as lesser beings. Yes, we are older and wiser, and our children are not fully mature, but they are still human beings uniquely created by God.

So when it comes to communication, be mindful of trying to control or rush them. Treat your children with respect, tenderness, and kindness, acknowledging their growth, level of maturity, and unique personality type. Aim to speak to your children when you are more self-aware, self-regulated, and able to attune to them and their needs. Of course, there will be bad days when you're far from that target and deep in your unhealthy communication style. Instead of falling into blame or shame, embrace grace and take the opportunity to repair your relationship by apologizing and reconciling.

When You're Not Doing Well

You can speak to your children in a demanding, insensitive, challenging tone. You enjoy confrontation because, to you, it feels like intimacy. You like it when others stand up for themselves and their beliefs and go toe-to-toe with you with equal intensity and passion. However, not all personalities enjoy confrontation, and your family can experience you as too intense, intimidating, quick to anger, and blunt. Remind yourself that you are God's Beloved Child, and so is your child. From this new place of awareness, you can begin to ask curious questions, becoming gentler and more patient when communicating your thoughts and decisions. Going forward, you can be more mindful of your tendency to come across as insensitive or task-driven and work to apologize and repair when necessary.

When You're Healthy

Your communication style is warm, honest, and generous, and you comfort your children with your confident presence. You accept others' viewpoints and gauge your intensity, dialing back your energy when you notice your approach makes someone uncomfortable. You realize that being too blunt and direct can hurt your children's feelings, so you take a softer tone, prioritizing kindness and patience. You encourage your family to honestly share their emotions with you.

Instead of denying your role in conflicts, you seek accountability, apologize, and repair. When your children make mistakes and stumble, as all people do, they know they can count on your loving protection and self-regulated assertiveness to help them find their way forward.

Steps Toward Parenting Growth

- Recognize your tendency to place circumstances out of your mind, forgetting or denying that they occurred.
  - To combat denial, pause and take a moment to reflect on your child's concerns. Then repeat what you've heard them say and accept the role you played in the situation.
  - "It sounds like you're saying my powerful voice made you feel scared. Is that right? I'm sorry. I want you to feel safe, and I can understand why you don't feel safe when I'm angry or intense."
- Find trustworthy people to help hold you accountable when you're too abrasive, intense, or not giving yourself a break.
  - Because you are assertive and a natural leader, you may believe you can handle everything on your own, but God created us to parent in a community. Connecting with other mothers exposes you to diverse perspectives, and you'll receive helpful feedback and much-needed support.
- Ask your family to gauge your intensity and tell you when they feel overpowered and need you to dial it back a bit. Resist the urge to argue or dismiss their observations.
  - Your family feels seen and valued when you hear their concerns and accept feedback. Take some deep breaths so your body can slow down and relax. Your family will notice your relaxed posture and will feel more at ease in your presence.

8

- Balance your courage, strength, and determination with good self-care.
  - You can push yourself too hard, which negatively affects your physical body. It's important to recognize that you are human. Your body needs rest and to be cared for just like everyone else's. Your children are both attuned to and physically connected to you, so they can also feel tired and overwhelmed when you're pushing forward and not taking necessary breaks.
- Embrace generosity and mercy, plowing a path for others with your strength. One of the greatest gifts you give your children is modeling how to use your gifts to help those less fortunate than you.
  - Some days, you must stand in front of your children to protect them from a world bigger and more complicated than they are ready to handle. Other times you can serve alongside them and bring about justice together.
- Put down your armor and reveal your vulnerability and tender heart. By modeling vulnerability, authenticity, and self-care, you show your children that it's okay to be imperfect and that vulnerability is a strength. This fosters a deeper and more meaningful bond.
  - "Mommy is feeling a little sad and tired right now. Yesterday was a hard day at work, and my boss said things that didn't feel good. Sometimes grown-ups feel upset and need help too, just like you. It's okay to talk about your feelings. In fact, it's really brave. We had a lot planned for today, but let's see what we can take off our list so we can rest."

Your Blind Spot

When you're around those you are most comfortable with (mainly your family), you'll display misaligned characteristics you will not easily recognize. Your family notices, but you are usually blind to them, and that is why we call them blind spots.* Being unaware of your blind spot characteristics can negatively affect your parenting and connection with your children. To become aware of your blind spot, ask yourself the following questions:

- Is there a part of me that believes I need to offer my help, support, and advice to receive love and affection from my family and friends?
    - To protect yourself from feeling vulnerable, you take on a protective role, seeking to be the one who provides support and help to others rather than asking for the support you need. Demonstrating your love through actions rather than verbal affection or emotional expression feels easier. However, this can become transactional and lead you to believe that receiving love depends on what you do for others.
- Do I hide my needs and emotions, fearing they will threaten my relationships and keep others from giving me affection and appreciation?
    - In your blind spot, you may ignore your own needs and focus on supporting and helping those you care about. Your needs are a sign of dependence on others, which you find challenging to accept because you are naturally self-sufficient, and opening up about your needs leads to vulnerability and the risk of being rejected or disappointed if they are unmet.
    - However, receiving support and care doesn't diminish

---

* If you're familiar with the Enneagram, you already know that your blind spot displays the average to unhealthy attributes of your Type 2 Path. If you're wondering what Type 2 has to do with Type 8, you can find out more in chapter 28, "Your Enneagram Internal Profile (EIP)."

8

your strength. It strengthens your bonds with loved ones, leading to a more balanced and fulfilling give-and-take in your relationships.

• Do I take offense when family and friends don't help and care for me in the same way I love and support them?
  – In your blind spot, you can subconsciously hope that others will pick up on your needs and reciprocate without your having to ask explicitly. When this doesn't happen, you feel hurt or disappointed. However, expecting people (especially your children) to read your mind is unfair.
  – Instead, clearly communicate your needs and expectations with your loved ones and recognize that different personalities have unique ways of showing love and affection that may not be exactly like yours.

• Do I assume that all my motives and actions are pure with no hidden agendas?
  – When making decisions or taking action, pause and ask yourself why you are doing what you're doing. Are you helping and protecting others to receive their appreciation? Are you trying to ignore your own needs? Do you want to maintain control?
  – These reasons will be hard to recognize in your blind spot and will take a lot of practice and self-reflection to bring to the surface. But by honestly examining your motives, you can develop more authentic relationships built on trust, respect, and genuine care.

AWARE (Mindfulness Exercise)

Awaken

Awaken to a thought or feeling. It could be:

- The belief that it's not okay to be vulnerable or to trust anyone.
- A fire in your gut that makes you want to stop this mindfulness exercise and confront someone or take control of something.
- A hidden desire to be cared for so you can carry a lighter load and experience a safe emotional connection.
- A specific story from your childhood.
- A worry about your parenting, your relationship with your child, or your child's future.
- Feeling sad or vulnerable or experiencing physical pain from being too hard on your body. (Pay attention to your body. Are your fists clenched? Do you feel tightness in your chest, a fiery feeling in your gut, or any aches and pains? Can you sense how unmoving and powerful your presence is even though you are trying to relax and soften?)

Welcome

Welcome and extend kindness to this part of you without guilt or shame. Remain curious, not critical. What starts as a thought is connected to a deeper feeling, and what begins as a feeling in your body has a story to share. Stay kind by remembering that this part of you has good intentions. It's trying to help you, even if it's causing you problems.

You can relax knowing that though you are weak, God is strong. He is here to save and protect you and will never betray you. He is your true Advocate, and because of his grace, you can welcome and show kindness to all the parts of your heart, including the wounded and vulnerable parts.

Ask

Ask God to help you interpret what this part of you is trying to communicate and the motives behind the thoughts and feelings.

8

How is this part of you connected to a wounding story from your childhood? Resist any urge to deny your vulnerable stories or shield your softer emotions. This can be difficult for Type 8s because you believe you should always be strong and invulnerable. However, just as connecting is the goal for parenting, connecting is also the goal for AWARE. Give this part of your story space to be seen and heard.

Receive

Receive the forgiveness and compassion God offers you, allowing him to help you guide this misaligned and hurt part of your heart back to the truth. Spend a few minutes reading truths like these verses about God's strength and protection:

- "Fear not, for I have redeemed you; I have called you by name, you are mine. When you pass through the waters, I will be with you; and through the rivers, they shall not overwhelm you; when you walk through fire you shall not be burned, and the flame shall not consume you. For I am the LORD your God, the Holy One of Israel, your Savior." (Isaiah 43:1–3 ESV)
- That is why, for Christ's sake, I delight in weaknesses, in insults, in hardships, in persecutions, in difficulties. For when I am weak, then I am strong. (2 Corinthians 12:10)
- The LORD himself goes before you and will be with you; he will never leave you nor forsake you. Do not be afraid; do not be discouraged. (Deuteronomy 31:8)

Engage

Engage yourself, your children, and your parenting in a new way, resting in the truth that God went to great lengths for you and is your Great Protector. From this newly aligned place, you can put down your armor, and your children will experience the same patience and gentleness you are learning to show yourself.

Prayer for Type 8 Parents

Gracious and loving God, thank you for my unique role as a Type 8 mother. I am grateful for my confidence, strength, and ability to plow a path for my family. I acknowledge that these qualities reflect your own heart. Thank you for allowing me to demonstrate your passion and strength.

I recognize that my desire to protect and bring about justice reflects you. At the same time, I acknowledge that in a fallen world, my desires can become misaligned and harmful. Forgive me for the times I've rushed after my goals and accidentally harmed others in my way. Thank you for satisfying my core longing to be protected and not betrayed so I can rest and let others see and care for my tender heart.

Grant me the strength to lead my family with wisdom and courage but also the humility to admit when I'm wrong and to learn from my mistakes. Help me see that true strength comes not from denying my weaknesses but from embracing them and growing through them.

Make me aware of my autopilot reactions that do not serve my children well so I can change how I engage with them. Thank you for showing me how to lead with love and understanding rather than dominance. Teach me to be emotionally present for my children, to listen to their needs and fears, and to be a source of comfort and support. Give me the strength to be vulnerable and open, even when it feels uncomfortable, so I can connect with my children on a deeper level.

When I feel the urge to control every situation and overprotect, remind me that I can trust you to take care of my family. Give me the wisdom to know when to stand firm and when to let go. Help me discern when to protect my children and when to allow them to face challenges and learn from their experiences. Fill me with your peace, knowing you go before us and will never betray us.

Please grow my community so I may find support, encouragement, and a sense of belonging in my parenting journey. I know my children

8

need connection and vulnerability just as much as I do, so give me the courage to connect with other families, even though I fear showing my weaknesses. Surround me with authentic, imperfect, and gracious mothers who appreciate my strength and encourage me to share my tenderness and needs.

As I vulnerably embrace my story and the wounded parts of my heart, help me parent my children from a place of new awareness. Fill me with patience, emotional connection, and the desire to repair the relationship. And keep my heart humble and open to gray areas so I can see my children as you created them to be and not how I want them to be. As I navigate the joys and challenges of parenting, grant me the gift of knowing when to pause so I can rest and connect with my inner world and family. Amen.

CHAPTER 25

Type 9: The Peaceful Accommodator

Thoughtful | Reassuring | Receptive |
Nonjudgmental | Accommodating | Resigned

Parenting Core Motivations

Your **Core Fear** is being in conflict, tension, or discord, feeling shut out and overlooked, or losing connection and relationship with your children.

Your **Core Desire** is to have inner stability and peace of mind in your parenting journey.

Your **Core Weakness** is sloth—remaining in an unrealistic and idealistic world and falling asleep to your passions, abilities, and desires by merging with others (including your children) to keep the peace, remain easygoing, and not be disturbed by your anger.

Your **Core Longing** is to hear and believe that "your presence matters." You feel that you need to diminish your presence to minimize conflict and maintain peace, but God is calling you to wake up, show up, and bless your family and the world with your full presence in how he created you to be.

Primary Parenting Perspective

To achieve your core motivations, your primary focus is to be warm, kind, loving, and focused on your family and friends. You easily

9

see everyone's point of view and accommodate others in order to keep harmony in relationships and maintain inner peace of mind. You struggle with inertia, and most of the time, you are not moving in your own right action, but instead, you are merging with other people's passions. You fundamentally believe that your presence, opinions, priorities, desires, and life do not matter much, and that you should not assert or promote yourself, so you decide to blend in or stay in the background.

Parenting on Autopilot

The autopilot response of all parents is to guide their children to become little versions of their type's personality, because it's easier to parent a child to be just like you! Becoming aware of this tendency is a big step toward changing course and parenting with awareness so that you can respect your children's unique personalities and valid perspectives.

As a Type 9, you want to raise "Little Peaceful Accommodators," children who exhibit calmness, gentleness, empathy, compassion, and independence. You prioritize nurturing your children to become well-mannered, composed, and respectful. You help them learn to pay attention to more than one side of an issue, avoiding unnecessary conflict whenever possible. You encourage your kids to foster an environment of peace and kindness. You envision your kids maintaining harmony for themselves and those around them.

While these are great qualities to teach your children, when parenting on autopilot, you can expect a level of calmness and respectfulness inconsistent with their developmental abilities. Children often have unregulated emotions and are naturally self-focused, making life chaotic, not peaceful. It takes time for their brains to develop the ability to look outside themselves and consider the needs and feelings of others. Furthermore, not all personalities will be as peaceful and composed as Type 9s. Knowing this can help you step back, parent with curiosity and grace, and allow your children to express their natural emotions or desires.

Parenting Style

You are patient and reassuring, and you bring a sense of calm and peace to any situation. Your children can freely share their thoughts and emotions without fear of judgment because you always show them kindness and grace. During your children's inevitable ups and downs, you remain a source of quiet strength and comfort. You can see all points of view and are a natural peacekeeper and agent of reconciliation.

However, you deeply desire independence and autonomy and prefer not to be bothered so you can experience inner peace. When life or people interrupt your peaceful state, you will try to accommodate them to keep the peace so you can quickly return to your inner calm. You don't often express your desires or feelings because you believe it will cause conflicts and discord, so you pretend you do not have your own preferences. This causes you to suppress your anger and to "go along to get along." When you try to satisfy your longing for harmony, connection, and comfort, you can become conflict-avoidant, indecisive, and quickly overwhelmed.

The work of parenting is often overwhelming, not only because of the physical labor but also because children have strong opinions and confident demands. This can trigger your core weakness of sloth—ignoring what you need and want so you can merge with your children's preferences to maintain peace. Appeasing your children may make them happy in the moment, but this dynamic can lead to anxiety. Even though your children loudly push against your boundaries, developmentally, they still need your steady leadership to feel safe and secure. Deep down, they want to be able to trust in your guidance and provision.

Internally, you struggle to believe your voice and opinions matter, so you become self-forgetting and self-belittling. You focus too much

9

on others and lose your identity, adopting others' thoughts, feelings, and agendas to achieve a false harmony. You fall asleep to yourself, yet you often have an internal frustration about being overlooked. This deep well of anger rarely comes out, but it erupts like a volcano when it does. You can become completely numb and deny your anger or be blind to how you express it (passive-aggressiveness, irritability, disassociation, passivity, and frustration). This inability to see the negativity of your actions affects others. It creates more distance in your relationships, causing the very conflict and disconnection you fear.

When you learn to take your struggles and longings to God, you can begin to awaken to your convictions, feelings, and passions. You believe that you matter and can make a difference in this world. Realizing that true peace comes from entering into conflict, not avoiding it, you genuinely engage with your family and friends and your own life. Then your harmonic nature can bring out the best in everyone, changing your family tree and making your home (and the world) a better place.

Levels of Alignment: Assessing Your Inner Well-Being

Aligned

Living in this healthy state, you become awake to yourself. Believing your voice and presence matter, you boldly pursue your calling and invest in your passions, using your gifts to bless your family and the world. Your strength and kindness inspire and comfort your children. You bring empathy and harmony to others but without merging with them in the process. In this balanced approach, you teach your children the importance of self-worth and living in alignment with one's true self and purpose. Your presence blends God's unwavering tranquility and gentleness with his firm, assertive strength.

Misaligned

Living in this autopilot state creates an inner fog, obscuring your thoughts, feelings, and desires. You often forget your value and feel that your presence doesn't matter. You view others as more significant, aligning with them to maintain peace by ensuring their happiness and seeking their affirmation and connection. Deep down, you hope your family recognizes your worth and reassures you of it. If they don't, feelings of devastation and invisibility emerge. Articulating these emotions becomes challenging because self-understanding is elusive, and you hesitate to enter conflict or risk a break in connection with others. Going along to get along is your mode of operation.

Out of Alignment

Living in this unhealthy state, you strive to accommodate everyone. You constantly focus on keeping others happy to maintain what feels like peace of mind and inner stability, losing yourself along the way. You neglect your personal growth and think your presence doesn't matter. A deepening inner fog makes you numb, causing you to fully merge with others, effectively becoming a doormat, letting others dictate how you live, think, feel, and parent. When mistreated, you offer no resistance (except for the rare emotional explosion that takes your family by surprise). This unchecked disassociation causes you to retreat within, bypass personal pain to keep the peace, and sideline your fundamental needs and desires.

Childhood Message

As a child, your mind was receptive and open, and you were very aware of the emotional tone of your family dynamic. You took on the expectations of your parents—consciously and unconsciously. Meeting your parents' wishes and demands caused you to become overwhelmed in trying to keep the peace and ensure everyone was happy. Instead of communicating your needs and frustrations, you withdrew to calmer spaces and retreated into your imagination, where you found peace, freedom, and autonomy. You kept a low profile to keep your home peaceful and didn't assert yourself or ask for too much. You felt like you needed to become invisible so that your presence did not add more conflict to your family. You believed being unseen would bring about peace, but what actually happened was that you became invisible to others. Sadly, you also lost touch with yourself.

Your childhood message is, "It's not okay to assert yourself." This was either directly said to you or is a message you perceived through interactions with others. It is hardwired in your mind, like a record player that constantly played when you were a child and continues to play into adulthood. It was painful then, and it is painful now. This message, however, is false. God says and demonstrates that your presence matters. Resting in this truth allows you to grow into your redeemed and free self, understanding that your full presence is crucial to the story he has planned for you as his Beloved Child.

Parenting Struggles and Relationship Issues

- You remain unaware of your anger (frustrations and irritabilities) and the passive-aggressive strategies you use to protect yourself. Instead of openly addressing issues, you can withdraw and say nothing, or you hide your feelings as you show frustration in your facial expressions. Your children can feel unvalued and try to accommodate your emotions, creating a similar dynamic to what you experienced growing up.

- You can unknowingly and unintentionally redirect your anger and frustration onto another person not involved in the original conflict. When you avoid conflicts at all costs, unresolved issues simmer beneath the surface. It feels safer to vent to someone uninvolved and who might not react as strongly. This can create a negative mood in your house because it's the only place you feel safe to vent. Your children will naturally blame themselves for your frustration, especially if it's leaking out on them.

- Your desire for peace and harmony can make you passive and reluctant to make decisions. When you procrastinate, issues can become more complicated, and you and your children miss out on opportunities. When you rely on others to make decisions for you, your parenting feels inconsistent. Your children might become confused about expectations and rules, affecting their sense of security and understanding.

- You can struggle to say no, even when you are overwhelmed, uninterested, or your gut tells you it's not in your or your child's best interest. It's important to step into assertiveness so your children can learn to stand up for themselves someday. If your child already has an assertive personality, defaulting to their preferences may bring peace in the moment, but it ultimately leads to insecurity because being in charge is too much for any child to carry.

- You unconsciously check out if something feels too large, difficult, or uncomfortable to handle. You distract and numb yourself by engaging in routine, familiar activities that require little effort or attention, giving you comfort. You can become irritated or disoriented if your children interrupt your comfy routine. When you avoid difficult conversations and complex problems, your children can feel frustrated or uncertain about where to turn for help.

9

Communication
Style

As parents, we can unknowingly look down on our children as lesser beings. Yes, we are older and wiser, and our children are not fully mature, but they are still human beings uniquely created by God. So when it comes to communication, be mindful of your tendency to check out when you're not doing well. Treat your children with respect, tenderness, and kindness, acknowledging their growth, level of maturity, and unique personality type. Aim to speak to your children when you are more self-aware, self-regulated, and able to attune to them and their needs. Of course, there will be bad days when you're far from that target and deep in your unhealthy communication style. Instead of falling into blame or shame, embrace grace and take the opportunity to apologize and repair.

When You're Not Doing Well

You meander in your talk style because you haven't taken the time to care for yourself and discover what you think and feel. You might say yes when you want to say no out of fear of conflict or upsetting someone, and you may agree to do something with no plans to follow through. You can be passive-aggressive and stubborn or check out and withdraw. When you find yourself in this unhealthy communication style, take a few deep breaths and let your body relax so your child sees that you have physically softened toward them. Remind yourself that you are God's Beloved Child, and so is your child. From this new place of awareness, you can begin to ask curious questions, increasing authenticity in your relationships, including your relationship with yourself. Going forward, you can be more mindful of your true desires and feelings and communicate them earlier to avoid frustration or resentment.

When You're Healthy

You honor how God made you by getting to know your thoughts and emotions. You embrace your passions and opinions, expressing yourself authentically and assertively. You model to your children how to resolve conflict by addressing problems, setting boundaries, and learning to say no instead of merging with others' preferences. This promotes a balanced and respectful family dynamic. When your children make mistakes and stumble, as all people do, they know they can count on your genuine presence and connection to encourage their growth.

Steps Toward Parenting Growth

- Realize that not all conflict is bad. Healthy conflict allows you to express your thoughts and needs, fostering a deeper connection with your family.
  - Addressing conflicts also teaches your children essential skills in communication, empathy, and conflict resolution. When you stop avoiding conflict at all costs, you can begin to experience the real, genuine peace you seek.
- Focus on knowing your perspective. Honor yourself by embracing your opinions and values. Type 9s have a lot under the surface.
  - Through journaling, you can explore your inner world and cultivate a stronger sense of self. When you realize you've agreed to something you don't actually want to do, be honest with yourself and your family.
  - "I'm sorry I got your hopes up. Sometimes I say yes to things because I want to make everyone happy, but I forget to think about what I really want. I'm trying to understand

219

myself more and communicate my wants and needs more
clearly. I want us all to have a great time, so let's talk about
other options and find something we can all enjoy."

• Recognize the deep frustration (anger) within you and express
it more quickly with emotional balance.

  – Stay attuned to subtle signs like physical tension or inner
frustration. When you notice these signs, take a few deep
breaths and practice naming your feelings and sharing
your thoughts out loud. Be assertive, clear, and direct. If
you've already taken your frustration out on your family,
apologize and repair.

  – "I want to talk to you about what happened earlier. I asked
you to clean the bathroom, and when I saw it was still a
mess, I felt like you ignored me and didn't care about me. I
should have talked to you, but I got angry and yelled. I'm
sorry for taking my frustration out on you. Can we talk
about why you didn't clean the bathroom and how you felt
when I got upset?"

• Become awake to your abilities, passions, and desires, and pursue them.

  – When was the last time you felt alive or deeply connected
to something? The answer to that question can help you
hone in on your passions and boost your self-confidence.
As you pursue your interests, you'll experience renewed
energy, allowing you to engage more with your family and
the world.

• Learn to unapologetically say no to others' requests. You will
get pushback from others, but you'll learn to respect yourself
and lovingly stand your ground.

  – Ask yourself, "Is this what I want to do?"

  – "That sounds like a lot of fun, and I appreciate the invitation.
However, my schedule is full right now, and I need to

prioritize some personal projects I'm working on, so I won't be able to make it. Let me know next time you go."

- Recognize when you are numbing out. Your avoidance is connected to your anger. It can manifest in binge-watching TV, overeating, getting overly involved in a hobby, doing meaningless chores, or zoning out and entering a fantasy land. Distracting yourself helps temporarily, and you may even convince yourself it's a form of self-care. However, your anger will keep simmering, and if you don't address the problem, it will eventually boil over and negatively affect your family.
  - Ask yourself, "Do I feel detached or disconnected from what's happening around me?" and "Do I feel like I'm on autopilot, just going through the motions?"

Your Blind Spot

When you're around those you are most comfortable with (mainly your family), you'll display misaligned characteristics you will not easily recognize. Your family notices, but you are usually blind to them, and that is why we call them blind spots.* Being unaware of your blind spot characteristics can negatively affect your parenting and connection with your children. To become aware of your blind spot, ask yourself the following questions:

- Do I ignore or suppress my emotions and identity so I can focus on achieving?
  - In your blind spot, achieving is not for your own fulfillment

---

* If you're familiar with the Enneagram, you already know that your blind spot displays the average to unhealthy attributes of your Type 3 Path. If you're wondering what Type 3 has to do with Type 9, you can find out more in chapter 28, "Your Enneagram Internal Profile (EIP)."

or personal growth but is a result of your tendency to merge with others' expectations and demands so you can avoid conflicts and maintain peace. As a parent, there will be many times you need to work hard for the benefit of your child, but you want to make sure you are also making time for self-care to pursue your passions.

– Ask yourself, "Do I feel unfulfilled or dissatisfied despite my achievements?" If your answer is yes, you are achieving for others at the expense of yourself.

• When someone exposes my weaknesses or failures, do I feel shame and believe I am worthless, incompetent, and not good enough?

– Your tendency to merge with others' expectations can make you overly sensitive to judgment, and you'll feel worthless when your vulnerabilities are pointed out. This exposure also threatens the peace you work so hard to uphold. In your blind spot, you can easily spin into shame, so take a deep breath and acknowledge the discomfort, then honor yourself and how you uniquely process information by asking for time to reflect.

– "Thank you for sharing your perspective with me. Let me take some time to reflect on what you've said. Can we reconnect later?"

• Do I people-please and overencourage to gain affirmation and value in the eyes of others?

– In your blind spot, you often take on a secondary role. You listen to others and downplay your own achievements or needs. Your family and friends affirm you for making them feel at ease and supported, and you can assume you've found your rightful place in a group. However, this results in you always being a secondary character and never the lead.

– Downplaying yourself does not honor the voice and abilities

God gave you. He affirms your true worth as his Beloved Child, so you can show up, assert yourself, and bless others with your full presence.

- Do I take on busywork to feel productive and look hardworking?
  - In your blind spot, you numb out by staying active. It appears to others that you are hard at work accomplishing important things. You may also brag about your efficiency to point out your value to your family and receive their praise. Really, you are just distracting yourself from more important matters like dealing with a conflict.
  - Ultimately, this habit can prevent you from fully engaging with your family and embracing meaningful moments. You end up overworked, exhausted, and stuck with the same problem you tried to avoid. The truly efficient approach is to honor yourself and your relationships by working through conflict.

AWARE (Mindfulness Exercise)

Awaken
Awaken to a thought or feeling. It could be:

- The belief that it's not okay to assert yourself.
- Feeling that your presence doesn't matter to your family or that you've been overlooked and not taken seriously.
- A desire to numb out, get in your comfy routine, and not be bothered by others.
- A specific story from your childhood.
- A worry about your parenting, your relationship with your child, or your child's future.

9

- A feeling of resentment, irritation, or internal fog. (Pay attention to your body. Does your face feel tense, or is anger simmering in your gut? Do you have an inability to find and organize your thoughts? When you reflect on recent conversations, were you smiling and nodding even though you didn't fully agree?)

Welcome

Welcome and extend kindness to this part of you without guilt or shame. Remain curious, not critical. What starts as a thought is connected to a deeper feeling, and what begins as a feeling in your body has a story to share. Stay kind by remembering that this part of you has good intentions. It's trying to help you, even if it's causing you problems.

You can relax knowing that your presence matters to God and his unfolding purposes. He has given you the unique ability to see all viewpoints and be nonjudgmental, and because of his grace, you can welcome and show kindness to all the parts of your heart.

Ask

Ask God to help you interpret what this part of you is trying to communicate and the motives behind the thoughts and feelings. How is this part of you connected to a wounding story from your childhood? Resist any urge to disconnect or numb out. This can be difficult for Type 9s because you value inner peace, and often, parts of your heart bring up events and feelings you'd like to ignore. However, just as connecting is the goal for parenting, connecting is also the goal for AWARE. Give this part of your story space to be seen and heard.

Receive

Receive the forgiveness and compassion God offers you, allowing him to help you guide this misaligned and hurt part of your heart back to the truth. Spend a few minutes reading truths like these verses about how God values, loves, and has a purpose for you:

- For we are God's handiwork, created in Christ Jesus to do good works, which God prepared in advance for us to do. (Ephesians 2:10)
- "Peace I leave with you; my peace I give you." (John 14:27)
- For the Spirit God gave us does not make us timid, but gives us power, love and self-discipline. (2 Timothy 1:7)

Engage

Engage yourself, your children, and your parenting in a new way from a heart resting in the truth that your presence and calling are vital to God's plan. From this newly aligned place, your children will cultivate the same confidence and self-awareness you are learning to develop in yourself.

Prayer for Type 9 Parents

Gracious and loving God, thank you for my unique role as a Type 9 mother. I am grateful for my thoughtfulness, warmth, and ability to foster reconciliation for my children. I acknowledge that these qualities reflect your own heart. Thank you for allowing me to demonstrate your peace and unity to my family.

I recognize that my desire for inner calm and stability reflects you. At the same time, I acknowledge that my desires can become misaligned and harmful. Forgive me for the times I've sought a false peace by over-accommodating and avoiding conflicts instead of honoring myself and my family by engaging and seeking resolutions. Thank you for fulfilling my core longing to be valued and vital to the world not just for my peacekeeping but also for my unique gifts and insights.

9

I often find myself in the haze of an internal fog, which obscures my true desires and prevents me from knowing myself. Please lift this fog so I can see how my path differs from others'. When I get lost in indecision and self-doubt, grant me the strength to take intentional steps forward. As I emerge from this fog, may I discover the beauty of my own identity and purpose, and may it shine brightly in my interactions with my family and in all aspects of my life.

Make me aware of my autopilot reactions that do not serve my children well so I can change how I engage with them. I know you didn't create me to always be a secondary, supportive character in my family and friend groups. Help me confidently take on the central role you have for me where my voice is heard and my passions are pursued. Let me be an inspiration to my children so they also learn to honor their individuality and boldly embrace their dreams. Thank you for giving my family unique personalities and purposes. Help us to work together without merging so we can bless each other and the world.

Thank you for giving me the gift of mindfulness and fostering peace and understanding. As I help my children find common ground and harmony in the world, may I also guide them to stand up for themselves and find their voice. Help me teach them the value of respectful communication, active listening, and the art of healthy compromise so they, too, may be examples of your peace.

Please grow my community so I may find support, encouragement, and a sense of belonging in my parenting journey. I know my children need connection just as much as I do, so give me the energy and mental clarity to connect with other families even when I feel my presence doesn't matter. Surround me with vulnerable, imperfect, and gracious mothers who equally invest in me, see my gifts, appreciate my voice, and encourage me to pursue my dreams.

As I vulnerably embrace my story and the wounded parts of my heart, help me parent my children from a place of new awareness. Fill me with confidence in my parenting abilities, clarity in my thoughts, and the desire to enter conflict and to repair. Keep my heart open to the immeasurable impact of my full presence in my children's lives. As I navigate the joys and challenges of parenting, grant me the gift of true peace that only comes from you. Amen.

9

CHAPTER 26

An Overview of the Nine Types of Children

Wouldn't it be great if you could type your children and understand why they do what they do and feel how they feel? Knowing a child's Enneagram type would completely transform your parenting, but unfortunately, that's not how it works. By this point, you know that even though children are born with their main Enneagram type, the full unfolding of their personality is still developing. On top of that, by nature, they mirror you. Much of what you see in your children is what they have observed from you, so in many ways, your children are teachers of *your* inner world.

Of course, there will be many times your children are complete mysteries to you, and their behavior is unexpected and utterly foreign to your personality. These, in fact, are glimpses into your child's unique inner world. When you know the Enneagram, it's tough not to see a specific personality type expressed in your child. However, it's important not to label your children, because only they can reveal their true motivations. The minute you type them, you limit their development into the people they were designed to be, and they can feel confused, unseen, or believe they must fill a predetermined mold. Just as you shouldn't raise your child to become mini versions of you, you shouldn't raise your child to become the Enneagram type you think they are.

So what should you do if you're not supposed to type your children? It's simple: do the same things you're learning to do with your own inner world. Be curious and welcoming, and pay close attention to what you're noticing. As you start to see patterns and unique traits, you can hold two or three Enneagram types loosely and approach your children from those perspectives to see what is helpful and makes them feel genuinely seen. But until your children are old enough (at least the teenage years) to discover and confirm their Enneagram type, you must live in the tension of uncertainty. Your assertive toddler, who you thought might be a Type 8, can become a child so obsessed with dinosaurs that you're sure she's a Type 5. But then she grows into an anxious preteen who seems more like a Type 6 and later morphs into a withdrawn, moody teenager who is undoubtedly a Type 4, except for the days she aces her exams and leads her soccer team to victory like a Type 3.

As you can see, typing other people is impossible because behavior isn't the standard. Motivations are, and only your child can reveal the why behind their behaviors. This will take time, because they're just getting to know themselves, and they are changing and growing every day. We all use all nine types to varying degrees, and this is especially true in children who are mirroring the changing world around them. This is part of the journey and joy of parenting. Each day is an opportunity to discover something new about your child as they learn about themselves and the world. As unique creations and Beloved Children, you both have much to learn and discover about yourselves and each other.

If you're new to the Enneagram, it can be difficult to hold two or three types loosely for your children while also trying to figure out your own main type. It's more important to stay focused on your inner world because, as you've learned in this book, healthy parenting has more to do with you than your child. Self-awareness forms the foundation for effective parenting. The Enneagram wasn't designed to change or fix other people. It's a framework for self-awareness and personal growth. By understanding your inner world, you'll create a nurturing and supportive environment that, in turn, fosters your children's growth and well-being.

As you're learning about yourself, speak truth over your children. Like most people, your children want to hear and believe all nine of the core longings, so tell them they are good, wanted, and loved for simply being themselves. Let them know you see them and notice how special and unique they are. Remind them that their needs are not a problem, that they are safe and secure, and that they will be taken care of and protected. Show them every day that their presence matters to you. Over time, you'll discover which core longings have greater meaning to your child.

The same is true for the other core motivations. All people share similar fears, desires, and weaknesses, but some are stronger than others. To help foster your curiosity in your younger children's developing personalities, here are each type's core motivations, written simplistically so you can easily use this language to form your own curious questions relevant to your unique children and their stages of life. Seeing the core motivations from this childlike style can guide you in communicating with your children so they can vocalize what is accurate and true for them.

Type 1

Core Fear

My Biggest Worry: I'm afraid of making mistakes, being bad, or not getting things perfectly right.

Interaction Example: "It's okay that you spilled your juice. Sometimes people feel scared when they mess up because they don't want people to think they are bad. Do you ever feel that way?"

Core Desire

What I Want: I always want to do the right thing, be a good person, and make correct and fair choices.

Interaction Example: "That looks great. I can tell you're trying hard to color in the lines. Do you feel really good inside when you get it just right?"

Core Weakness

My Greatest Challenge: I tend to hold in and not want to express my feelings of frustration or anger, but I often feel very upset inside when things are not perfect.

Interaction Examples: "Sometimes people get really upset about things not being perfect. Did you feel angry when you didn't do well on your spelling test? Did you say any mean things to yourself?"

"I've noticed you talk a lot about your sister's messy room. Do you ever feel frustrated at her for not picking up? How do you think it should look?"

Core Longing

What I Really Need to Hear from Others: "You are a good person."

Interaction Examples: "You were created with so much goodness. I see your thoughtful heart and how you always try to do what's right. I love that about you, but do you sometimes wish you could have more fun?"

"Remember, it's okay to make mistakes. You don't have to be perfect to be good. I love you just the way you are."

Children of this type often desire to be the 'good boy' or 'good girl' by doing things correctly and accurately. They fear being seen as bad, evil, and wrong. You might notice your child having a strong inner critic, taking their responsibilities seriously, and often striving for perfection. They might advise others on how to be more organized or correct, and they can sometimes seem more like a little adult.

Healthy Characteristics:

- Extremely responsible and diligent in schoolwork and chores.
- Sets high standards for themselves and others, promoting excellence.
- Strives to be fair and just, resolving conflicts fairly.

Average Characteristics:

- Can be critical of themselves and others, leading to perfectionism.
- May struggle with rigidity and an inability to adapt to changes.
- Tendency to be overly rule-bound, causing stress and tension.

Unhealthy Characteristics:

- Prone to outbursts of anger and frustration when perfection is not met.
- Overly judgmental of others, leading to strained relationships.
- Experiences constant anxiety due to the fear of making mistakes.

Type 2

Core Fear

My Biggest Worry: I'm afraid of being rejected, unwanted, too needy, and unworthy of love if I'm not helpful enough.

Interaction Examples: "Sometimes people feel scared that others won't like them unless they are helpful and do things for them. Do you ever feel that way?"

"I've noticed you're helping your brother with his homework a lot lately. Are you afraid you won't be important to him if you say no?"

Core Desire

What I Want: I always desire to be appreciated, loved, and wanted by others.

Interaction Example: "I really appreciate you helping me wash the dishes. Does it make you feel good inside to help me? Helping people does feel good. How do you think you would feel if I forgot to say thank you?"

Core Weakness

My Greatest Challenge: I deny my own needs and emotions and try to discover how I can help others so I can receive their gratefulness and love.

Interaction Examples: "You always seem to know exactly what your friends need. I bet they really love how much you care about them. But do you ever wish your friends would notice what you need?"

"Do you ever feel tired when you're helping people and wish you could stop? I want you to remember that you are important and your feelings matter. It's okay to say no and do things for yourself."

Core Longing

What I Really Need to Hear from Others: "You are wanted and loved."

Interaction Example: "You have such a caring and helpful spirit. I love that about you. I want you to know that I love you and want you all the time, not because of the things you do for me but because of the amazing person you are. I love you no matter what."

These children strongly desire to be liked, wanted, and loved and fear being rejected, unwanted, and unloved. You may notice your child being empathetic, often helping others before addressing their own needs. They might get their feelings hurt easily and seek to please others, sometimes manipulating situations to gain approval. Teachers may often find them to be good students.

Healthy Characteristics:
- Warm, empathetic, and supportive in relationships.
- Always ready to help friends and family in times of need.
- Creates a sense of belonging and connectedness in their community.

Average Characteristics:
- May become overly involved in others' problems, neglecting their own need.
- Can be manipulative at times to gain approval or attention.
- May feel unappreciated and hurt when others don't care for them in the same ways.

Unhealthy Characteristics:
- Becomes manipulative and controlling to maintain a sense of importance.
- Struggles with codependency and neglecting their needs in relationships.
- Develops resentment and anger when they feel unappreciated.

Type 3

Core Fear

My Biggest Worry: I'm afraid people will think I'm worthless, unpopular, and a failure.

Interaction Examples: "Sometimes people feel scared that they won't be good at things. Do you ever feel that way?"

"You've been practicing really hard on your free throws. It's good to practice the things you really love to do. But I wonder if you're also worried your teammates and coach won't like you as much if you miss a shot. Is that true?"

Core Desire

What I Want: I want to be admired, successful, popular, and valuable.

Interaction Example: "I'm so proud of you. It's nice to stand out and be recognized for all your hard work. How did you feel when you won the spelling bee?"

Core Weakness

My Greatest Challenge: I try to become someone other people will like and admire, and sometimes I forget who I really am.

Interaction Example: "I noticed you haven't practiced the piano lately, and you're spending more time playing video games with your friends. Video games are fun, and I'm glad you have friends to play them with. But it's also important to remember the other things you love to do. You don't have to win your friends' approval by being just like them. You are amazing just as you are."

Core Longing

What I Really Need to Hear from Others: "You are loved and valued for simply being you."

Interaction Examples: "You were created with so many amazing talents, and I love watching you win. But guess what I love even more! I love it when you're silly and having fun just being yourself."

"I'll always support you, but I want you to know that I love you for who you are. In fact, if you never won another award, I would love you just the same."

Children of this type desire to appear successful and admirable, and they fear being a failure or being seen as incompetent. You might observe your child constantly striving to accomplish tasks successfully, excelling in various interests, and being quite confident. They often present themselves well, both in appearance and in their achievements.

Healthy Characteristics:

- Highly motivated and goal-oriented, achieving success in various areas.
- Self-confident, capable, and a role model for others.
- Inspires and motivates peers with affirmations and encouragements.

Average Characteristics:

- Becomes overly focused on external achievements, neglecting personal values.
- Can be competitive, sometimes at the expense of others.
- May struggle with balancing their desire to achieve and personal needs.

Unhealthy Characteristics:

- Obsessed with success, leading to a sense of emptiness and burnout.
- Becomes image-conscious and willing to compromise ethics for success.
- Experience a fear of failure that paralyzes them from taking risks.

Type 4

Core Fear

My Biggest Worry: I'm afraid I'm not special enough for people to notice me and that I'm somehow defective or flawed. I fear others will not let me feel my deep emotions.

Interaction Examples: "Sometimes people compare themselves to others and feel scared that they're not as special. Do you ever feel this way?"

"I noticed you looked a little sad with your friends. Do you sometimes feel like you're missing something they have? Like they're really good at things or have something special about them, and you're worried you don't?"

Core Desire

What I Want: I want to be unique and special and to express my authentic self.

Interaction Example: "You are so unique and special, and I love how you're never afraid to share your emotions and be your true self."

Core Weakness

My Greatest Challenge: I often wish I had what others have because I feel like they have qualities I lack.

Interaction Example: "You seemed upset after your sister shared that she got the lead role in the play. Sometimes I feel envious and wish I were like someone else because I think they are better or have what I'm missing. Is this how you're feeling toward your sister?"

Core Longing

What I Really Need to Hear from Others: "You are seen and loved for exactly who you are—special and unique."

Interaction Examples: "I want you to know that even when I seem busy, I always see how unique and special you are. I love you exactly the way you are, and I'm so glad I'm your mom."

"I love hearing about your deep feelings and thoughts. I'll always be here to support and try to understand you no matter what you're experiencing."

These children strongly desire to be unique and authentic and fear being plain or mundane. Your child may see the world in a unique way, get deeply affected by their emotions, and sometimes feel "different" or "flawed" compared to others. They might be drawn to artistic and creative pursuits and tend to live in a more melancholy state at times.

Healthy Characteristics:
- Expresses creativity and uniqueness in various aspects of life.
- Emotionally deep and introspective, fostering meaningful connections.
- Has a keen sense of empathy and understanding for others.

Average Characteristics:
- Can be moody and self-absorbed, seeking validation for their emotions.
- Prone to melancholy and self-pity during difficult moments.
- May have difficulty letting go of past wounds.

Unhealthy Characteristics:
- Exaggerates their feelings and emotions for attention.
- Develops a sense of victimhood and isolation from others.
- Experiences intense jealousy and envy of others' happiness.

Type 5

Core Fear
My Biggest Worry: I'm afraid people and the world will overwhelm me with their expectations, and I'll run out of energy or not have the knowledge or resources I need.

Interaction Examples: "Sometimes people are scared they won't have what they need. Do you ever worry you won't know what to do or say, or won't have something you need?"

"That was a long day. I'm sorry if it felt like we did too much.

Sometimes, when I'm tired, I feel like I have a battery inside me that's almost out of power. I usually feel better after I spend some time alone. Do you ever feel that way?"

Core Desire

What I Want: I desire to know a lot of things and feel capable and competent.

Interaction Example: "You are so smart, creative, and capable. I'm confident you can handle whatever comes your way this school year."

Core Weakness

My Greatest Challenge: I feel like I lack what I need, and hanging out with people too much will drain me, so I keep to myself and hold on to my things to minimize my needs.

Interaction Examples: "Do you sometimes feel like you need to keep to yourself because too much time with the family makes you feel drained?"

"Are you afraid you'll run out of your favorite paint color? Is that why you're having a hard time sharing with your brother?"

Core Longing

What I Really Need to Hear from Others: "Your needs are not a problem."

Interaction Examples: "It's okay to take time for yourself to recharge alone. I understand you need that, and I'm sorry if I made you feel it was wrong. God made you special that way, and he loves to be with you in your quiet place and meet your needs."

"I want you to know that sharing your thoughts and feelings with me is always okay. Your needs are never a problem, and I love to help you."

Children of this type desire to understand everything so they can feel capable and competent. They fear that too much social interaction with

239

others will lead to being depleted of all their inner resources and energy. You might notice your child seeking a great deal of alone time so they can recharge and process their thoughts and feelings. They ask profound questions and are naturally curious. They often observe from a distance and can be introverted, preferring solitude to group activities.

Healthy Characteristics:
- Intellectually curious and insightful, seeking to understand the world.
- Respectful of personal boundaries and privacy in relationships.
- Offers valuable knowledge and expertise to friends and peers.

Average Characteristics:
- May withdraw from social situations to avoid emotional demands.
- Can become overly focused on accumulating knowledge at the expense of experiences.
- Struggles with sharing thoughts and emotions and appearing distant.

Unhealthy Characteristics:
- Becomes emotionally detached and isolated from others.
- Hoards information and knowledge, feeling superior to others.
- Experiences paranoia and fear of intrusion into their privacy.

Type 6

Core Fear
My Biggest Worry: I'm afraid of feeling afraid and being all alone with no one to help guide me and keep me safe. I worry that people will blame or abandon me.

Interaction Examples: "Sometimes people feel alone and scared that no one will help them or show them the way. Is this how you felt today at your new school?"

"Accidents happen, and I know you and your friends didn't mean to break our neighbor's window with your ball. But can we talk about why you didn't want to tell me? Sometimes people worry they'll be blamed and left out of a group. Were you afraid your friends would be upset with you if you told me?"

Core Desire

What I Want: I want to feel secure and have loyal, supportive people in my life who can guide me toward safety and security.

Interaction Example: "You are so brave to go to summer camp. I know you're going to have a great time. Your first year can feel a little scary because it's a new experience. I'll make sure you have everything you need, and we'll talk about what to expect before you leave. Your camp counselors will be there to guide and support you, and I'm only a phone call away."

Core Weakness

My Greatest Challenge: I struggle with worry, and I'm always trying to predict and prevent bad things from happening.

Interaction Examples: "Did you remind me of the speed limit sign because you're worried we might get in an accident? Thanks for looking out for us. It's okay to relax. I'll watch for the signs so you don't have to."

"I know you're worried about the debate competition. It's hard to look forward to something when you think of all the bad things that could happen, and having all that attention on you can feel like a lot of pressure. You're great at debate. You can trust yourself and the skills God gave you."

Core Longing

What I Really Need to Hear from Others: "You are safe and secure."

Interaction Example: "I know worries pop up sometimes. That's a normal part of life. Just remember that you have family and friends who care about you and will be there to help you when you need it. God loves you so much, and he's always with you, guiding and protecting you too. You're never alone."

These children desire safety and security. They may seek reassurance, guidance, and loyalty from friends and family but will sometimes play the devil's advocate in discussions. They can have a restless, worrying mind that envisions multiple negative scenarios that they need to plan for and prevent from happening. However, they struggle with trusting themselves and feel they need guidance and support. You will see that their loyalty and commitment to others is a prominent trait.

Healthy Characteristics:
- Trustworthy and dependable, providing stability to relationships.
- Offers support and loyalty to friends and family in times of need.
- Carefully considers all possible outcomes and is an excellent troubleshooter.

Average Characteristics:
- Tends to be anxious and cautious, anticipating potential problems.
- Seeks reassurance and validation from others to alleviate fear.
- Can be skeptical and sometimes overly critical.

Unhealthy Characteristics:
- Experiences intense anxiety and paranoia, imagining worst-case scenarios.
- Becomes distrustful and accusatory, straining relationships.
- Feels overwhelmed by fear and struggles to make decisions.

Type 7

Core Fear

My Biggest Worry: I'm afraid of feeling trapped in sadness and inner emptiness, so I try not to be bored or miss out on experiencing something fun.

Interaction Examples: "Sometimes people are scared to feel sad because it feels like they might get trapped in their sadness and they won't know how to escape. Do you ever feel that way?"

"I'm sorry you have to miss the party. When I miss an event, I sometimes feel left out and bored. I worry I'm missing all the fun. Is that how you feel?"

Core Desire

What I Want: I want to have fun and feel happy and fully satisfied.

Interaction Example: "I see your love for excitement and new experiences. I'm here to support your adventurous spirit and help you create fun opportunities when I can. Your desire for joy is a wonderful part of who you are."

Core Weakness

My Greatest Challenge: When I slow down, I often feel empty inside and try to fill myself with fun experiences, hoping I'll feel complete and content.

Interaction Examples: "Do you remember how excited you were to get your bike? Wouldn't it be nice if that feeling lasted forever? I wonder if you're asking for a new scooter because you want to feel that excitement again. Do you think that might be true?"

"When we make spaghetti, we drain the noodles in the pot with the holes. Do you ever feel like you have one of those pots inside you, and no matter how much fun you have, you always need more because your joy is leaking out, and you don't want to feel empty?"

Core Longing
What I Really Need to Hear from Others: "You will be taken care of."

Interaction Examples: "I love that God gave you a spirit that loves to explore and have fun. Did you know he's with you in all your adventures? And when you're bored or feeling sad, he can fill up the spaces inside you that sometimes feel empty."

"I love to take care of you. No matter what happens or where life takes you, you can count on me to be there for you."

Children of this type desire happiness, new experiences, and fun and fear missing out on something enjoyable. You might see your child as optimistic, outgoing, and always seeking new adventures. They resist boredom and mundane tasks. They enjoy a variety of exciting experiences but sometimes struggle with discipline, focus, and follow-through.

Healthy Characteristics:
- Enthusiastic and fun-loving, spreading joy to those around them.
- Seeks adventure and embraces new experiences with optimism.
- Resilient in the face of challenges, finding opportunities in adversity.

Average Characteristics:
- May avoid facing difficult emotions through constant distractions.
- Struggles with commitment and discipline, always seeking novelty.
- Can become impulsive and overindulgent in pursuit of pleasure.

Unhealthy Characteristics:

- Escapes from emotional pain through excessive distractions or addictive behaviors.
- Struggles with dissatisfaction and a constant need for more excitement.
- May become reckless, endangering themselves and others.

Type 8

Core Fear

My Biggest Worry: I'm afraid of being weak and powerless and people controlling me or taking advantage of my big heart.

Interaction Examples: "Sometimes people want to be in control because they fear someone might hurt them or their feelings. Do you ever feel this way?"

"I'm sorry you didn't get team captain. Following someone else's lead is hard when you're a natural leader. I'm wondering if you feel powerless right now. What do you fear will happen to the team if you're not captain?"

Core Desire

What I Want: I want to protect myself and my close friends and family.

Interaction Example: "Thank you for looking out for your little sister and always protecting her. She feels so safe when she's with you. I love watching you use your strength for good."

Core Weakness

My Greatest Challenge: I know what I want and am not afraid to get it, even if it means pushing myself too hard or bossing others around to get what I want.

Interaction Examples: "Remember at the park when all your friends wanted to play hide-and-seek, but you demanded they play tag with you instead? How do you think your friends felt about that? Do you think they felt you were being too bossy and pushy?"

"I understand you want more control over your curfew. The rule is in place to keep you safe and help you get enough rest. We can discuss this and come to a compromise, but I need you to be respectful and not talk over me or make demands."

Core Longing

What I Really Need to Hear from Others: "You will not be betrayed."

Interaction Examples: "I want you to know it's okay to feel weak and need help. You're human, and all humans have weaknesses. In fact, admitting when you're weak or sad is sometimes the strongest and bravest thing you can do."

"I'm here to protect you and take care of you. I never want to let you down, but I know I'm not perfect, and I'll make mistakes. In those moments, you can trust that God's love for you never fails. His love is like a strong wall that keeps you safe."

These children desire strength and fear being controlled or at the mercy of injustice. Your child may exhibit strong, assertive energy and tend to stand up against perceived injustices, even if it means intervening physically. Underneath their tough exterior, they often have a soft and tender heart.

Healthy Characteristics:
- Assertive and protective, standing up for justice and fairness.
- Offers support and strength to those in need, demonstrating vulnerability.
- Trusts their instincts and intuition, making decisive choices.

Average Characteristics:

- Can be argumentative and domineering to assert control.
- Struggles with vulnerability and may suppress emotions.
- May develop a fear of being controlled, leading to resistance.

Unhealthy Characteristics:

- Becomes aggressive and confrontational, intimidating others.
- Suppresses emotions to maintain a tough exterior, leading to inner turmoil.
- Constantly needing to be in control and will challenge and confront others to get what they want.

Type 9

Core Fear

My Biggest Worry: I feel afraid when people are upset with each other, and especially when they are upset with me, because I don't want to be overlooked or lose connection with those I love.

Interaction Examples: "Sometimes it feels scary when other people aren't getting along. You might worry that they will stop caring about each other. Do you feel this way sometimes?"

"It's okay if you'd rather watch instead of play the game with us. But I wonder if, deep inside, you do want to play but don't feel comfortable joining in because we have big emotions when we play a game, which might feel like we're mad at each other. When we get loud and competitive, how does that make you feel inside? We'd love for you to play with us. How can we help you feel more at ease and comfortable?"

Core Desire

What I Want: I want to feel calm and peaceful.

Interaction Example: "I've seen how important it is for you to feel calm and peaceful. It's like having a cozy blanket around your heart. When I'm around you, I feel comfortable and happy too."

Core Weakness

My Greatest Challenge: I stay in my daydreams where everything is easy and happy so I can blend with others and maintain peace. I go along to get along with others, but this makes me forget what I like and want.

Interaction Examples: "I noticed you didn't say anything to your sister when she raided your closet. Sometimes people hide their feelings because they want to keep things peaceful. Are you afraid of upsetting your sister if you say your feelings out loud?"

"Joining the same activities as your friends sounds like fun because you'll get to spend a lot of time together. But I wonder if you're doing too much of what they enjoy and forgetting about what you're great at and love doing. Is that true?"

Core Longing

What I Really Need to Hear from Others: "Your presence matters."

Interaction Examples: "I want you to know that you are important to me, and I love when you share your thoughts and feelings with me. Your presence adds a special kind of happiness to our family."

"You were created for a specific purpose, and I can't wait to see the amazing things you will do."

Children of this type desire peace and fear conflict of any kind. You may notice your child striving to keep things pleasant, avoiding conflict by not voicing opinions. They can be accepting and adaptable but may also become overly accommodating or stubbornly resistant when pushed. These children are kind, thoughtful, and nonjudgmental. They often have a calm, peaceful energy and seek comfort through close relationships.

Healthy Characteristics:
- Able to express themselves in a calm and assertive manner while keeping relationships harmonious.
- Values peace and cooperation, mediating conflicts with tender strength and kindness.
- Offers a sense of stability and support to loved ones.

Average Characteristics:
- Avoids conflict at all costs, even at the expense of personal needs.
- May struggle with indecision and passivity, going along with others.
- Can become complacent and disengaged in their own life.

Unhealthy Characteristics:
- Suppresses emotions and opinions, leading to a sense of numbness.
- Experiences chronic avoidance and a fear of assertiveness.
- Becomes passive-aggressive and distant in relationships.

CHAPTER 27

The Dance

The Dance was created to show the relational dynamics between two Enneagram types and is typically used to bring awareness to marriage dynamics. However, the concept can be used with any relationship, including parent-child relationships. This tool is most helpful when you know both people's Enneagram types, so if you have adult children interested in the Enneagram, The Dance can give you great insight into why you keep running into the same conflicts over and over again. If you have younger children who have not yet discovered their Enneagram type, you can still apply The Dance principles to help you break free from the unhealthy communication cycles you often repeat.

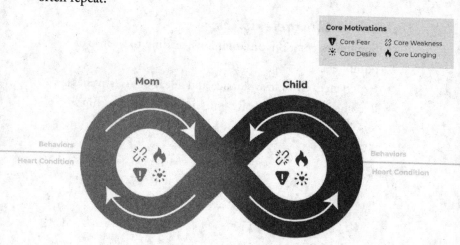

The infinity loop shows the emotional and behavioral dynamics of a relationship. Each person is connected and influences the other.

You'll notice a line through the infinity loop. Below the line is what is internally happening in each of your hearts. Above the line is the observable behaviors. In any conflict, the observable behaviors are easy to judge, and when you don't consider the inner motivations, you can make assumptions or, in the case of children, punish behaviors without understanding the deeper thoughts and emotions that caused the response in the first place.

To help you see how this dynamic works, here is an example using a Type 2 mom and a Type 4 child:

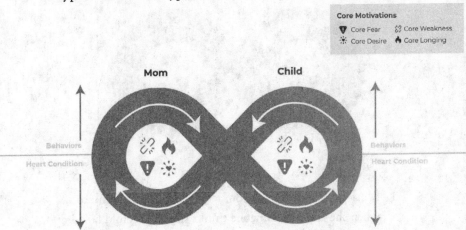

1. Mom fears being unwanted, unloved, and not needed, so when she assumes her child does not want or need her . . .

2. She finds areas in her child's life that need her help, opinions, or advice and then inserts herself in "helpful" ways so her child acknowledges his need for her.

3. The Type 4 child interprets mom's actions as signifying he is inadequate and flawed without her help.

4. The child either withdraws and becomes distant or becomes emotionally reactive. He feels he must fully process his emotions before they can move forward.

In this scenario, the child withdrawing or becoming emotionally reactive toward his mom further activates the mom's core fear of being unwanted, unloved, and unneeded, and the cycle repeats.

Here's another example using a Type 3 mom and a Type 9 child:

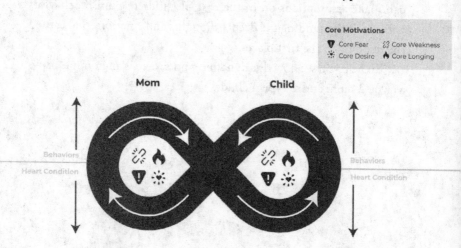

Core Motivations

🜚 Core Fear   ⟲ Core Weakness
☀ Core Desire   ♠ Core Longing

Mom   **Child**

Behaviors   Behaviors

Heart Condition   Heart Condition

1. Mom fears appearing incompetent and unsuccessful, so when she assumes someone thinks she or her child failed or was inadequate in some way . . .
2. She makes new goals, plans, and tasks to ensure she and her child become better versions of themselves.
3. The Type 9 child interprets her mom's actions as saying she is never good enough.
4. The child either tries to over-accommodate to please her mom or loses heart by disengaging and numbing out.

In this scenario, the mom could feel like her core desire is being met if her Type 9 child accommodates her wishes, but this is at the expense of the child and further causes the child to fall asleep to her own opinions and desires. If the child disengages instead, this will further activate the mom's core fear of being unsuccessful, and around and around they go.

In both examples, each reaction activates the other person's core fear, causing them to react. It's common for people to continue in this unhealthy cycle until they tire, resolving nothing. The same issue will then continue to pop up and cause them problems. But by understanding how this cycle begins, you can also learn to end it by pausing long enough to consider what's going on beneath the surface (the deeper motivations within you and your child).

If you have younger children, you only have half of the information because your child has yet to confirm their type, which means you don't yet fully know what motivations are activating them. This is okay because the most important part of the equation is *you*. Your goal is to stop the cycle, and since your child is too young to stop it on their end of the infinity loop, you must stop it on your end by becoming aware of your own misaligned thoughts and emotions that are sabotaging the relationship.

When you find yourself in an unhealthy dance, ask yourself one of these questions:

- What triggered my reaction? Is this really about my child's behavior, or something else?
- Can I give myself a moment to breathe and collect my thoughts before responding?
- Am I tired, hungry, or stressed, and is this influencing my response to my child's behavior?
- What emotions am I feeling right now? Can I name them and understand where they're coming from?
- Are my expectations for my child realistic, given their age and development?
- Can I remind myself that my child's behavior doesn't define them or my worth as a parent?

- What are some positive aspects about my child that I can focus on at this moment?
- Can I remind myself that it's okay to make mistakes and learn with my child?
- How would I want someone to react if I were in my child's shoes?
- Can I see the situation from my child's perspective?

When you ask yourself questions like these, you're no longer focused on outward behaviors. You're looking below the surface, and this change in perspective gives you more compassion. Your child will notice you soften toward them, which helps them begin to calm down as well. You can then ask your child curious questions:

- Do you want to talk now or have some time to yourself?
- How are you feeling? Can you use words to tell me?
- Where do you feel your emotions in your body? Can you point to them?
- What happened that made you feel like this?
- Sometimes drawing or writing about your feelings can help. Want to give it a try?
- Can you tell me what I did that hurt your feelings? You can be honest with me.
- Let's take a deep breath together. It can help us both feel better.
- How about we go outside? A change of scenery can help.
- What would you like to do instead? Let's try to find a compromise.
- If there's one thing you wish could change right now, what would it be?

Reflecting on these questions in the moment can be difficult, especially when you don't have a lot of time. It's beneficial to revisit these lists frequently, familiarizing yourself with the questions so they become readily accessible even during tough times. Asking yourself just one question can significantly shift your perspective, helping you approach the situation and your child from a less anxious heart. Furthermore, the questions you ask your child show that you care about their perspective and feelings. You're no longer just parenting; you're nurturing a relationship that will flourish as your child grows.

In the same way that your emotional well-being influences your child, the health of your marriage also affects their overall happiness and security. If you are married, we recommend using The Dance to strengthen your relationship with your spouse. Even if you try not to fight in front of your children, they still pick up on underlying tensions and negative emotions between you and your partner. A healthy marriage creates a stable foundation for your entire family. For more details, visit www.becomingus.com and read our book *Becoming Us: Using the Enneagram to Create a Thriving Gospel-Centered Marriage*.

CHAPTER 28

Your Enneagram Internal Profile (EIP)

If you're more familiar with the Enneagram, you already know that it is like an onion with many additional layers not included in this book. The decision to simplify the Enneagram was purposeful, because parenting is complicated enough on its own, and the last thing I want you to feel is overwhelmed. What I hope you've felt throughout this book is "enough." You are enough. God chose you to be your child's mother. You're the right and best person for the role. Furthermore, he is within you and is more than enough to fill you with discernment, self-awareness, confidence, and peace so you can make the right choices for your children and be fully present and at ease in your most important relationships—with yourself, your family, and God.

As you continue in your parenting journey, there will be seasons when you have the space to dive deeper into your desire to know yourself more fully so you can bring even more awareness and transformation to yourself and your family. For those days, I've included this summary of a concept YEC has created called your Enneagram Internal Profile (EIP).

EIP reveals that you are more than just one number (or type). Your main type is the driving force behind why you think, feel, and behave the way you do, but it is not the only part of you that influences your life. As briefly discussed earlier, working alongside your main type are a variety of other Enneagram numbers that you're connected to. This may sound complicated, but you've already experienced these parts of your heart when you say things like, "There is a part of me that thinks or feels this is the best choice, but another part of me thinks or feels something different."

It's easy to categorize ourselves as one choice between two things, especially in our worst parenting moments. We are either good or bad, happy or sad, mean or nice. Yet we all know plenty of instances when we can be both happy *and* sad, like when our child bravely walks into school for the first time. We are complex people with many competing thoughts, feelings, and behaviors. When one part of us is thinking or feeling one way, another part of us can be thinking and feeling the complete opposite!

You can think of the EIP parts as family members. Every family member has their role—sometimes expressed in healthy ways and at other times unhealthy—but everyone has a role. In the same way, your EIP shines a light on the unique parts connected to your type, revealing how they interpret and interact with the world.

We've already introduced the concept of your Beloved Child and Wounded Child parts of your heart. These are the two parts of your main Enneagram type. The Beloved Child is the rightful leader of your heart. It tenderly listens, cares, and guides each part of your heart back to alignment. But allowing your Beloved Child to lead is difficult because you easily forget who you are and whose you are. When your Beloved Child is removed from leadership, other more unhealthy parts of your heart will step in. This shift in leadership (even if subtle) causes your heart to become misaligned with truth, which introduces chaos, confusion, anxiety, anger, fear, and shame.

Your misaligned parts don't intend to cause you more problems. They are trying to protect your Wounded Child. They represent coping strategies you've turned to since childhood. They helped you navigate a broken world during your most vulnerable times, but they are not mature leaders. Your Beloved Child is the rightful leader of your heart. The EIP will help you keep your Beloved Child in the driver's seat of your heart so that all the misaligned parts can find healing, alignment, and rest.

The Enneagram symbol maps out the parts influencing your thinking, feelings, and reactions. Below, you will find an example of your type's EIP. When you're ready to dive deeper into the Enneagram, we hope you'll check out our book *More Than Your Number: A Christ-Centered Enneagram Approach to Becoming A.W.A.R.E. of Your Internal World*. Understanding your internal map will help you recognize when you're veering off your healthiest path so you can pause and realign yourself with the truth.

Type 1 EIP

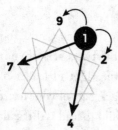

Wounded Child

Type 1's Wounded Child believes it's not okay for you to make mistakes and that you are bad, corrupt, and irredeemable.

Beloved Child

Type 1's Beloved Child says, "I don't have to be perfect to be good. I can relax and find the beauty in gray areas and imperfections."

Misaligned Parts

- Type 9 Wing—Blinds you from your inner critic, creating a lack of self-awareness.
- Type 2 Wing—Inserts you into others' lives to fix their flaws and mistakes.
- Type 4 Path—Focuses on your flaws and believes no one understands how right you are.
- Type 7 Path—Encourages rebellious, indulgent behavior to satisfy repressed cravings.

Aligned Parts

- Type 9 Wing—Gifts you with warmth, compassion, and empathy.
- Type 2 Wing—Gifts you the ability to come alongside others to offer help, not criticism.
- Type 4 Path—Gifts you with creativity and beauty within your order and logic.
- Type 7 Path—Gifts you with joy, freedom, and a sense of adventure so that you're not confined to limiting beliefs.

Type 2 EIP

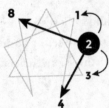

Wounded Child

Type 2's Wounded Child believes it's not okay to have needs of your own, and that you are unloved, rejected, and dispensable.

Beloved Child

Type 2's Beloved Child says, "I am deeply wanted and loved for who I am and not for my helpfulness and service."

Misaligned Parts

- Type 1 Wing—Inserts you into others' lives because you know what they need.
- Type 3 Wing—Focuses on image management and showcases all the good you do for others.
- Type 8 Path—Becomes reactive, challenging, and defensive when accused.
- Type 4 Path—Creates a victim mentality because no one understands you, and desires someone to rescue you.

Aligned Parts

- Type 1 Wing—Gifts you with wisdom and direction when helping others.
- Type 3 Wing—Gifts you with efficiency and practicality and honors your self-care.
- Type 8 Path—Gifts you the strength to plow a path for others and recognizes your inherent self-worth.
- Type 4 Path—Gifts you the ability to honor others' uniqueness and offer emotional support without fixing them.

Type 3 EIP

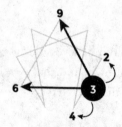

Wounded Child

Type 3's Wounded Child believes it's not okay for you to have your own feelings and identity and that you are worthless, inefficient, and a failure.

Beloved Child

Type 3's Beloved Child says, "I am loved for being me. I do not need to perform or become someone else to earn love."

Misaligned Parts

- Type 2 Wing—Dependent on people's opinions and inserts you into the lives of others to be a hero.
- Type 4 Wing—Believes no one will understand how difficult it is to maintain your image and achievements.
- Type 6 Path—Worries about what can go wrong and avoids trying for fear of failure.
- Type 9 Path—Avoids self-awareness to remain productive and on task.

Aligned Parts

- Type 2 Wing—Gifts you the ability to recognize needs and offer help as a coach and mentor.
- Type 4 Wing—Gifts you with creativity, emotional authenticity, and depth.
- Type 6 Path—Gifts you with the courage to move forward, be a team player, and accept failures.
- Type 9 Path—Gifts you the ability to bring your true self to the forefront and find rest.

Type 4 EIP

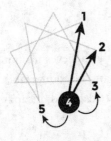

Wounded Child

Type 4's Wounded Child believes it's not okay for you to be too much and not enough and that you are defective, insignificant, and ordinary.

Beloved Child

Type 4's Beloved Child says, "I am complete and a special and unique creation. Therefore, I can be seen and loved for who I truly am."

Misaligned Parts

- Type 3 Wing—Focuses on image management to draw attention to how special and unique you are.
- Type 5 Wing—Observes and withdraws from the world to avoid appearing defective.
- Type 1 Path—Criticizes the aesthetics around you and judges others' emotional depth.
- Type 2 Path—Is manipulative and controlling of intimate relationships to win affection.

Aligned Parts

- Type 3 Wing—Gifts you with confidence in your unique talents so you can bless others.
- Type 5 Wing—Gifts you with intellectual insight and emotional depth to produce original works.
- Type 1 Path—Gifts you with groundedness, direction, productivity, and emotional balance.
- Type 2 Path—Gifts you the ability to focus on others and move toward them with an empathetic heart.

Type 5 EIP

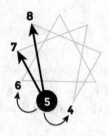

Wounded Child

Type 5's Wounded Child believes it's not okay for you to have needs and be comfortable in the world and that you are depleted, incapable, and ignorant.

Beloved Child

Type 5's Beloved Child says, "It is okay for me to take time for myself and rest and recharge, and I also have everything I need within me to confidently take the next step forward."

Misaligned Parts

- Type 4 Wing—Withdraws to avoid obligations and believes no one will respect your boundaries.
- Type 6 Wing—Is suspicious, reclusive, and insists on intense investigations before moving forward.
- Type 7 Path—Tries to get everything accomplished in a hyperactive and unproductive manner.

- Type 8 Path—Protects boundaries with intensity so others don't deplete you.

Aligned Parts

- Type 4 Wing—Gifts you with a balance of intellect and emotional depth, which fuels your inventiveness.
- Type 6 Wing—Gifts you with the courage to act and the loyalty to collaborate.
- Type 7 Path—Gifts you with optimism and new opportunities for yourself and others.
- Type 8 Path—Gifts you with the confidence and assertiveness to share your knowledge.

Type 6 EIP

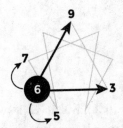

Wounded Child

Type 6's Wounded Child believes it's not okay for you to trust or depend on yourself and that you are in danger and abandoned.

Beloved Child

Type 6's Beloved Child says, "I am never completely alone or abandoned. My inner discernment gives me clarity, guidance, and support."

Misaligned Parts

- Type 5 Wing—Withdraws from others to find direction through anxious research.
- Type 7 Wing—Procrastinates, distracts, and tests the loyalty of others.

- Type 3 Path—Manages your image to find allies and look accomplished.
- Type 9 Path—Keeps you in comfortable routines to numb your fears.

Aligned Parts

- Type 5 Wing—Gifts you with self-confidence so you can move forward in life.
- Type 7 Wing—Gifts you a willingness to take risks and be less dependent on others' opinions.
- Type 3 Path—Gifts you with energy to move through self-doubt and engage with others.
- Type 9 Path—Gifts you a non-anxious, peaceful presence so you and others can rest.

Type 7 EIP

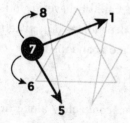

Wounded Child

Type 7's Wounded Child believes it's not okay for you to depend on others for anything and that you are limited, deprived, missing out, and will never feel content.

Beloved Child

Type 7's Beloved Child says, "I can be satisfied, content, and feel deep gratitude for all I have in this moment."

Misaligned Parts

- Type 6 Wing—Demands loyalty and is dependent on others in response to feelings of self-doubt.

- Type 8 Wing—Resists feedback from others and encourages you to do what you want.
- Type 1 Path—Is critical toward you and others when you are feeling deprived.
- Type 5 Path—Isolates you and makes you less reflective to avoid pain.

Aligned Parts

- Type 6 Wing—Gifts you with true loyalty and commitment to others and helps you finish what you started.
- Type 8 Wing—Gifts you with confidence and a groundedness in reality.
- Type 1 Path—Gifts you with principles to guide you, a clear focus, and a sense of responsibility.
- Type 5 Path—Gifts you with self-awareness and honesty and calms your reactionary tendencies.

Type 8 EIP

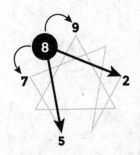

Wounded Child

Type 8's Wounded Child believes it's not okay for you to trust or be vulnerable with anyone and that you are controlled, betrayed, and vulnerable.

Beloved Child

Type 8's Beloved Child says, "Vulnerability is a strength, and I am worthy of rest. I can pause, reveal my big heart, and allow others to lead alongside me."

Misaligned Parts

- Type 7 Wing—Deflects others from trying to control you by using humor or spontaneity.
- Type 9 Wing—Represses your needs and desires and is less self-reflective and more private.
- Type 5 Path—Isolates you and focuses on gaining resources so you are less dependent on people.
- Type 2 Path—Inserts you into others' lives to hear how helpful and kind you are.

Aligned Parts

- Type 7 Wing—Gifts you with optimism, joy, and the ability to see the good in others.
- Type 9 Wing—Gifts you a nonjudgmental presence and the ability to create a safe place for others.
- Type 5 Path—Gifts you with wisdom and self-reflectiveness.
- Type 2 Path—Gifts you with the initiative to plow a path for others in need.

Type 9 EIP

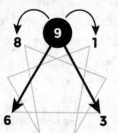

Wounded Child

Type 9's Wounded Child believes your presence doesn't matter, you shouldn't assert yourself, and you must go along to get along.

Beloved Child

Type 9's Beloved Child says, "My presence matters, and my voice is important. I was created for a special purpose."

Misaligned Parts

- Type 8 Wing—Resists and challenges others to back off and leave you alone.
- Type 1 Wing—Tells you how to do things better so you don't lose connections with others.
- Type 6 Path—Predicts what could go wrong and manages relationships to make sure everyone is happy.
- Type 3 Path—Focuses on your image so you can perform and please others.

Aligned Parts

- Type 8 Wing—Gifts you with the passion, drive, and intensity to get started.
- Type 1 Wing—Gifts you with more focus, precision, and efficiency.
- Type 6 Path—Gifts you with loyalty, secure relationships, and bravery amid fear and doubt.
- Type 3 Path—Gifts you with confidence and assertiveness to show up in life and bless others.

Conclusion

Thank you for journeying with me through the pages of this book. As you use these tools, please remember that there are no quick fixes, no formulas to figure out, and no mountain of motherhood perfection you must summit. There is also no time limit. Parenting is a journey. It doesn't matter what stage of parenting you are in; it's never too late. Whether you have preschoolers or grandchildren, there is always time to parent with more awareness and repair past harm. As you become more aware and at home with yourself and your parenting, please stay connected with us. I can't wait to hear your stories, struggles, and wins so I can help and encourage you along the way.

Let's connect!

Website: www.EnneagramForMoms.com
Instagram and Facebook: @yourenneagramcoach
Podcast: *Your Enneagram Coach, the Podcast*
YouTube: www.youtube.com/yourenneagramcoach
Find a certified Enneagram Coach: www.myenneagramcoach.com
Become a certified Enneagram Coach:
www.yourenneagramcoach.com/bec

"Peace I leave with you; my peace I give you. I do not give to you as the world gives. Do not let your hearts be troubled and do not be afraid." (John 14:27)

Acknowledgments

To Jeff, my husband and partner in every sense, I offer my sincerest thanks. Your unwavering encouragement for me to embrace my true self has been a gift beyond measure. Your love and support are the pillars of my world. I am eternally grateful for the friendship, love, and shared dreams that weave our lives together in work and play. Also, to my beloved children, Nathan and Libby McCord, I want to convey my appreciation for your incredible kindness, patience, and wholehearted embrace of the lessons we've embarked upon learning over the years. Your presence is a genuine gift and blessing in my life.

To my cherished family, including Dr. Bruce and Dana Pfuetze, Jerald and Johnnie McCord, and Dr. Mark and Mollie Pfuetze, you are the bedrock of love and unwavering support, providing us with a solid foundation to fulfill our calling. I hold deep respect and honor for each of you, acknowledging the profound love you've showered upon us. Thank you for generously permitting us to share our stories, allowing us to illuminate the love of God and the transformative power of the Enneagram.

A heartfelt appreciation goes to the exceptional team at Your Enneagram Coach. Your instrumental role in amplifying the heart of our pastoral ministry to thousands around the world is a gift beyond compare.

I extend my gratitude to our esteemed Leadership Team—Robert Lewis (chief strategy officer), Justin Barbour (chief financial officer), Christy Knutson (chief marketing officer), Adam Breckenridge (director of coaching), and Jane Butler (graphic designer). Your leadership is invaluable. And to our other team members—Alyssa Ramsey (executive assistant), Jessica Gormong (customer experience manager), Libby

McCord Christianson (social media manager), Nate McCord (podcast producer), Brian Lee (coaching & product), and Josh Earl (email manager). Your contributions are the backbone of our success.

To my collaborative writers, Lydia Craig and John Driver, your significant roles in organizing and refining this message to moms everywhere are immeasurable. Your patience, creativity, and professionalism have elevated our story. Our partnerships continue to blossom into dear friendships, and this book owes its existence to your invaluable contributions.

A heartfelt thank you to my literary agents at Wolgemuth & Associates—Robert Wolgemuth, Andrew Wolgemuth, Erik Wolgemuth, and Austin Wilson—for your partnership, wisdom, and diligent efforts in finding the perfect home for this vital project.

Gratitude overflows for the outstanding team at W Publishing Group (Thomas Nelson, HarperCollins Christian), my esteemed publisher. Your support is instrumental in spreading this important message worldwide.

About the Author

Beth McCord is an accomplished Enneagram speaker, author, coach, and teacher with over two decades of dedicated experience. Her passion lies in helping individuals and families rewrite their life stories, empowering them to realize that lasting change and meaningful relationships are possible. Beth's mission led to the creation of the Your Enneagram Coach community—a nurturing space where individuals can safely explore the Enneagram.

As a recognized Enneagram leader, Beth has honed her expertise through extensive training and certifications under renowned experts. Today, she simplifies Enneagram insights from a faith-based perspective, making it accessible to people from all walks of life. Her contributions extend globally, having trained over 2,500 coaches, authored twelve Enneagram books, and reached millions through her free Enneagram assessment and podcast.

About the Collaborators

Lydia J. Craig was born in Pennsylvania, grew up in Ohio, and now lives in Nashville with her husband and three kids. In the second grade, she fell in love with reading and writing, which led her to pursue her MLIS in library science and work as a librarian in local history and higher education. Along with creating children's stories to share, she enjoys reading, yoga, true-crime podcasts, TV shows featuring history and lost treasures, and working as the content writer for Your Enneagram Coach with Beth McCord. You can follow her writing journey at lydiajcraig.com.

About the Author

John C. Driver is a husband, volleyball dad, writer, and minister. He has authored, coauthored, or served as the primary collaborative writer for over thirty award-winning books, including the satirical *Ultimate Guide for the Avid Indoorsman* (Harvest House) and *Not So Black and White: An Invitation to Honest Conversations About Race and Faith* (Zondervan). A former history teacher who has been featured on *Good Morning America* (GMA3) and numerous other shows and podcasts, he earned a BA in history and an MS in curriculum and instruction from the University of Tennessee, Knoxville. John lives near Nashville with his wife and daughter.

Notes

1. Daniel J. Siegel, MD, and Mary Hartzell, MEd, *Parenting from the Inside Out: How a Deeper Self-Understanding Can Help You Raise Children Who Thrive* (New York: Jeremy P. Tarcher/Penguin, 2003 & 2014), 31.
2. Siegel and Hartzell, *Parenting from the Inside Out*, xi.
3. Siegel and Hartzell, *Parenting from the Inside Out*, 10–11.
4. Siegel and Hartzell, *Parenting from the Inside Out*, 18.
5. Groundbreaking work by Richard Schwartz speaks to this concept in his development of Internal Family Systems, in Richard C. Schwartz and Martha Sweezy, *Internal Family Systems Therapy*, 2nd ed. (New York: The Guilford Press, 2020). Becky Kennedy also applies IFS to parenting in her book *Good Inside*.
6. Alison Cook and Kimberly Miller, *Boundaries for Your Soul: How to Turn Your Overwhelming Thoughts and Feelings into Your Greatest Allies* (Nashville: Thomas Nelson, 2018), 27.
7. Daniel J. Siegel and Tina Payne Bryson, *No-Drama Discipline: The Whole-Brain Way to Calm the Chaos and Nurture Your Child's Developing Mind* (New York: Bantam Books, 2014), 111.
8. This is the central premise of *How Children Raise Parents: The Art of Listening to Your Family* by Dan B. Allender (Colorado Springs, CO: WaterBrook Press, 2005).
9. Siegel and Hartzell, *Parenting from the Inside Out*, 34.
10. Biola University, "Curt Thompson: Children and the Developing Mind," YouTube video, 5:43, August 22, 2013, https://www.youtube.com/watch?v=FNy_UGUOm5I.
11. Hunter Clarke-Fields, *Raising Good Humans: A Mindful Guide to Breaking the Cycle of Reactive Parenting and Raising Kind, Confident Kids* (Oakland: New Harbinger Publications, 2019), 63.

12. Becky Kennedy, *Good Inside: A Guide to Becoming the Parent You Want to Be* (New York: HarperCollins, 2022), 80.
13. Clarke-Fields, *Raising Good Humans*, 13.
14. Siegel and Hartzell, *Parenting from the Inside Out*, 54.
15. Kennedy, *Good Inside*, 33.
16. Clarke-Fields, *Raising Good Humans*, 14.
17. Clarke-Fields, *Raising Good Humans*, 14.
18. Hebrews 12:2.
19. Jerry Bridges, *The Discipline of Grace* (Colorado Springs, CO: NavPress, 1994 & 2006), 15.
20. Brennan Manning, *The Ragamuffin Gospel* (Colorado Springs, CO: Multnomah Books, 1990), 25.
21. Adapted from Ken Sande, *The Peacemaker: A Biblical Guide to Resolving Personal Conflict* (Grand Rapids, MI: Baker Books, 2004), chapter 6.